MW01156848

Boards that Matter

Building Blocks for Implementing Coherent Governance® and Policy Governance®

Linda J. Dawson and Randy Quinn

ROWMAN & LITTLEFIELD EDUCATION

A division of

ROWMAN & LITTLEFIELD PUBLISHERS, INC.
Lanham • New York • Toronto • Plymouth, UK

Published by Rowman & Littlefield Education
A division of Rowman & Littlefield Publishers, Inc.
A wholly owned subsidiary of The Rowman & Littlefield Publishing Group, Inc.
4501 Forbes Boulevard, Suite 200, Lanham, Maryland 20706
http://www.rowmaneducation.com

Estover Road, Plymouth PL6 7PY, United Kingdom

British Library Cataloguing in Publication Information Available

Library of Congress Cataloging-in-Publication Data

Dawson, Linda J., 1952–
Boards that matter : building blocks for implementing coherent governance and policy governance / Linda J. Dawson and Randy Quinn.
p. cm.
ISBN 978-1-61048-318-6 (cloth : alk. paper) — ISBN 978-1-61048-319-3 (pbk. : alk. paper) — ISBN 978-1-61048-320-9 (electronic)
1. School boards. 2. School board–superintendent relationships. I. Quinn, Randy. II. Title.
LB2831.D293 2011
379.1'531—dc22 2011008098

∞™ The paper used in this publication meets the minimum requirements of American National Standard for Information Sciences—Permanence of Paper for Printed Library Materials, ANSI/NISO Z39.48-1992.

Printed in the United States of America

Contents

Foreword

Good governance is everyone's business. The directions that organizations take and the outcomes they pursue, often with scarce resources, impact each one of us. This impact is felt especially when the organizations are public, or when they pursue some greater good: think schools, cities, counties, universities, colleges, and major nonprofits. These entities utilize funds that are provided by citizens or donors, and the work they do affects the lives of these citizens and contributors—and literally everyone else—in remarkable ways.

Governed and administered well, these organizations and institutions can be superbly beneficial and effective. Students are educated, the public is safe, communities are attractive, people in need have help. Without good governance, these same entities continue to exist and consume resources, but they are not nearly as effective. Students graduate but cannot comprehend. Bureaucracies expand while services decline, and those in need go without.

The purpose of Coherent Governance® is to provide a framework within which boards can effectively and efficiently govern the organizations for which they are responsible. In my three-plus decades of working with governing boards, I have come firmly to believe that school boards, city councils, county commissions, university and college regents, and major nonprofit boards are comprised of incredible individuals who give significant amounts of their time, energy, and ability in order to make a difference.

Unfortunately, so many of these good people labor within systems that are antiquated, dysfunctional, disjointed, and incoherent. As in so many areas of life, the right tool, the right model, the right framework can make a huge difference. Coherent Governance® is most certainly one of those tools.

I first met the developers of Coherent Governance®, Randy Quinn and Linda Dawson, through our common training in Policy Governance®—that remarkable model of governance developed by Dr. John Carver. Recognizing that his model needed advocates and accomplished practitioners, Carver began personally training others about the nuances of the model through his Policy Governance Academy™. With this training and a firm handshake and best wishes, John would send his trainees out to improve the governance world. Randy and Linda were trained in this way, as was I, along with my colleagues in *OnTarget Governance*, Carol Gabanna and Catherine Raso.

My own motive in attending the Academy as a CEO was purely mercenary. I was the City Manager of Bryan, Texas (the birthplace of Texas A&M University), and my incredible mayor and City Council had asked me to help them in their quest for good governance. We had seen and heard John Carver at a Texas Municipal League conference, and were mesmerized by how reasoned his approach was. Long before PowerPoint took center stage, John sat on a tall stool and drew crude pictures on a flip chart and held us captive with his insight into the struggles of balancing policy and administration. The council adopted Policy Governance®, and tasked me with becoming an expert.

Policy Governance® literally changed my life. Not only did it transform my CEO role, but I ultimately became a consultant in the model and co-authored *OnTarget Board Member—8 Indisputable Behaviors,* an allegorical fable that highlights Policy Governance. I also served as chair of the International Policy Governance Association, and more importantly, developed relationships that sharpened my thinking in each of these arenas.

Randy and Linda are two of the most influential consultants in the field. When I was recruited for and accepted the position of city manager in Denton, Texas (home of the University of North Texas and Texas Woman's University), I immediately encouraged my great mayor, Dr. Euline Brock, to utilize Randy and Linda to conduct a City Council retreat and governance workshop. Their unique blend of incredibly sharp intellect, coupled with unsurpassed charm, wit, and charisma, paved the way for Euline's terms as mayor to be especially successful. Her endorsement of Randy and Linda says much:

> Aspen principals are extremely talented facilitators and trainers. Their work with the Denton City Council has been superb. They are especially skilled in helping the council understand its role in developing outcomes and designing a process for such a diverse group to focus . . . thorough in their preparation and always exceed our high standards . . . understand the demands of leading in the public sector . . . never fail to make that easier to do. (Euline Brock, Mayor, Denton, Texas)

Of course, Randy's and Linda's true love is school boards. Their background at the Colorado Association of School Boards serves them incredibly well in this venue. They know schools from the inside out. They "get" the challenges of governing in a fishbowl, where a large segment of the owners often are disengaged and uninterested, while the rest of the owners are passionate and fixated because they have children in the district (making them customers as well). In fact, Coherent Governance® was developed in large part to deal specifically with the challenges governing boards face in this difficult arena.

John Carver always has been incredibly rigorous—as he should be—in his expectation that boards maintain strict integrity of the principles of Policy Governance®. At the same time, he has always encouraged his acolytes to find "the next best way."

While there are distinct differences between Policy Governance® and Coherent Governance®, the implementation strategies discussed in this book are critical to the success of any board launching its practice of either model. As a result of their having introduced, guided, and coached an incredible array of boards through successful governance adoptions, Randy and Linda provide a wholly workable framework for you—whether this is your first board experience or you are a longtime pro.

I guarantee that you will find the implementation strategies recommended in this book to be not only a breath of fresh air, but an easily followed roadmap leading to your board's long-term success in this new venture into good governance.

Enjoy your journey!

Mike Conduff
President and CEO, The Elim Group
Denton, TX, USA
Past President, International Policy Governance Association

Preface

The fact that you are reading this book likely indicates that your board has adopted either Coherent Governance® or Policy Governance®, and now is concerned with properly implementing the model. Or it could mean that your board has made an attempt at implementation, and is frustrated with the challenge to do it "correctly."

We know how you feel.

Both Coherent Governance® and Policy Governance® are extraordinary tools to help boards govern well, based on sound principles and common-sense logic. But only if a governing model is implemented in a meaningful way can it deliver on its promise of good governance. Otherwise, it can be more frustrating than helpful. It actually can become an impediment, rather than a useful tool for good governance.

Without some type of roadmap that indicates what to do, when, and how, proper implementation can be a daunting challenge for boards unaccustomed to the discipline of doing their own work and using such a well-defined system. Boards are required to do things they have never done, and the things they have done they must do in sometimes dramatically different ways. New and different skills are required, and higher levels of personal and group discipline are necessary—if the model is to provide the degree of added value the board envisioned when its journey toward good governance began.

But proper implementation doesn't have to be a death-defying experience. There are some very sensible, easily accomplished strategies that both boards and their CEOs can follow to take their model from the abstract to the real, and make it work as a well-oiled machine.

We refer to this as the "putting it on the ground and making it roll" stage. It is the fun part of transitioning from a board's having no defined way to get its work done to a logical, planned process for leading the organization for which the board is responsible, at an unprecedented level of effectiveness.

This book is a "how to" implementation training manual for boards that have adopted either Coherent Governance® or Policy Governance®. Although we will offer a very brief overview of the two models in chapter 1, it is assumed that the reader has some working knowledge of one or both of the models, and is concerned more with proper implementation than with understanding the model.

For readers who do not have some working knowledge of either of the models, we recommend first reading our book *Good Governance Is a Choice,* which will set a base for greater understanding of the procedures and strategies recommended in this book.

Throughout this book, we use the terminology of Coherent Governance® rather than Policy Governance®. For readers who are more familiar with Policy Governance terms, the translation from Policy Governance to Coherent Governance should be an easy one. The labels used for the four quadrants of policy are distinguished as follows:

EXHIBIT 0.1

Policy Terms in CG and PG

Policy Quadrant	**Coherent Governance**	**Policy Governance**
One	GC: Governance Culture	GP: Governance Process
Two	BCR: Board/CEO Relationship	GMC: Governance Management Connection
Three	OE: Operational Expectations	EL: Executive Limitations
Four	R: Results	E: Ends

Readers will note that many of the examples and references used throughout this book come from the world of school boards and public education. That is a deliberate choice for two very good reasons. Our dominant client base is public school boards, and thus our supply of good examples is greater from that field.

But equally important in our decision to use school board examples is our realization that everyone is familiar with public schools. All of us are or have been affiliated with them as students, parents of students, or if nothing else, a part of their "ownership," since we all pay taxes for their support. Public education may be one of the most challenging of all environments in which to implement a dramatically different governing model. Our belief is that if it can be done here, it can be done anywhere.

As with most ventures, there is no single way to do anything, but the recommendations we offer in this book are based on processes and systems that we know will work. They are an outgrowth of our fifteen or more years of work with boards using these governing models. All recommended processes are in use today by boards across the United States and internationally.

A client once told us that if he wanted twenty different answers to a single question, he would ask twenty different consultants. He wasn't far off. We have no quarrel with consultants who offer different insights and recommend different processes. They come from different places with different experiences, and their recommendations may work for them.

We express our deep admiration of and appreciation to our many clients whose work is the foundation for this book. Many of them eagerly have participated in some trial-and-error ventures that ultimately established workable processes and systems that this book now shares with readers throughout the world. Their perseverance and determination to succeed, sometimes against great odds, is inspirational.

Our objective is to make a difficult job as manageable and user-friendly as possible. Changing cultures, agendas, internal reporting processes, protocols, and literally almost everything else isn't easy.

Change does not come without challenge. But faithful implementation, we believe, positions the board to provide leadership in ways that it never before has experienced and aligns the entire organization to achieve its vision and Results.

Acknowledgments

We would like to thank our clients who have contributed much of the work shared in this book as examples. Some of these examples are attributed directly to those boards and organizations that created them, while others are left unidentified, usually for obvious reasons. Some examples are not attributed due to the interval between their creation and this book's publication, and the wholesale changes in personnel during the intervening years.

We extend our sincere gratitude to the following specific boards and organizations, not only for giving us the opportunity to coach their governance work, but also for their acceptance of the challenge to elevate their own performance as demonstrated by the quality work they have produced and their willingness to allow us to share it with readers throughout the world.

- Aspen, Colorado, School District
- Austin, Texas, Independent School District
- Columbus, Ohio, Public Schools
- Eden Prairie, Minnesota, Public Schools Board of Education
- Enduris of Spokane, Washington
- Fairfax County, Virginia, Public Schools
- Harrison, Colorado, School District 2
- Horry County, South Carolina, Public Schools
- Issaquah, Washington, School District 411
- Nikkei Concerns of Seattle, Washington
- Palm Springs, California, Unified School District
- Racine, Wisconsin, Unified School District
- San Diego, California, Unified School District

Chapter 1

Governing Models

Models are just that: models. They provide a framework for the board to do its job, and to express clear expectations for organizational performance. We frequently refer to governing models as operating systems for boards. Models are not ends in themselves, but rather they are a means to a much larger and more important end: good governance. They provide a systematic framework intended to position boards to organize their work and to lead their organizations in some coherent fashion.

On occasion, consultants and others refer to a "traditional" governing model. Actually, for most boards, this isn't a model at all; it is the *absence* of a model. Too often, governance is a cobbled-together mix of practices based on tradition. Processes used by most boards typically are reflections of the personalities currently serving on the board, along with that of the CEO.

In our experience, there are only two true, complete governing models: our own Coherent Governance® and John Carver's Policy Governance®. Some boards use features of both models, and attach other names to the resulting hybrid.

In order to qualify as a full-form model, we believe the system must be policy-based; must cover the full range of board responsibilities; must have form and structure sufficient to drive complete organizational alignment; must be designed to focus both board and staff on organizational results; and must eliminate role confusion by establishing clear lines of delegation and strict accountability.

Both Policy Governance® and Coherent Governance® have form and structure that hold the separate parts together in a coherent whole. Both models are policy-based systems driven by values, enabling boards to effectively lead the organizations for which they are responsible, making decisions that are theirs to make at the policy level.

Both models feature a small number of policies, usually not more than thirty or so, total. The policies are grouped into four quadrants, each serving a distinct purpose.

The real value of using either Coherent Governance® or Policy Governance® is that both models are based on principles experts long have recognized as being characteristics of effective boards. While both models may require board behaviors that are very different from the customary behaviors of many boards, they are very consonant with the behaviors *expected* of all boards. They are, in the truest sense, vehicles to enable boards to actually perform the way boards are intended to perform.

Some boards and board members resist the idea of adopting anything that has to do with a "model" or any organized governance system. They resist any structure they think may limit their individual freedoms or inhibit their ability to provide off-the-cuff direction to the organization.

For a board to attempt to govern effectively with no defined operating system is akin to playing a team sport without a set of rules or a game plan. On occasion, it may work. But more often than not, confusion, disappointment, and frustration are the results, rather than organizational progress.

Sometimes organizational success may be achieved in spite of the board, rather than because of it. But typically, organizational performance is no better than board performance.

In most organizations, good governance doesn't exist unless the board deliberately creates it. A coherent governing model, based on fundamental principles and values, can allow the board to build something greater than itself, enabling members to leave a legacy of visionary leadership for those members and staff leaders who follow.

The following paragraphs very briefly describe the two models that are the focus of this book, John Carver's Policy Governance® and our own Coherent Governance®. No attempt is made here to offer full descriptions of either model. Readers are expected to have a working knowledge of one or both models. For those who do not, we suggest Carver's *Boards That Make a Difference* as a source for Policy Governance information, and our own *Good Governance Is a Choice* for more information about Coherent Governance.

POLICY GOVERNANCE

Policy Governance® is a registered service mark of John Carver. Carver introduced this model to the world in the 1980s with the publication of his first book, *Boards That Make a Difference*. Policy Governance is based upon a set of traditional principles that people long have recognized as standards that good boards strive to practice. Carver recognized the difficulty that boards have in actually practicing those principles, and created his model to enable boards to effectively lead, direct, inspire, and control organizations through carefully crafted policy statements based on the principles.

The Policy Governance® board sets policy and rigorously monitors organizational performance for operational compliance and for outcome progress. The policies are grouped into four categories:

Ends: Ends policies define organizational products and outcomes for specified beneficiaries. They clearly state the "bottom line" the organization is expected to achieve over time: What benefit? For whom? At what cost?

Executive Limitations: EL policies set clear limits and controls on operational decisions that the board would find unacceptable. They define the boundaries within which the CEO and staff may operate. All EL policies are stated prohibitively, and serve to limit CEO authority.

Governance Process: GP policies define the board's own work and how it will be carried out. They clearly state the expectations the board has for itself, for the chair, for individual members, and for collective board behavior, including behavior at board meetings and for any board committees.

Governance-Management Connection: These policies define the specific delegation of authority to the CEO, a process and timeline for CEO evaluation, and accountability of the CEO.

Since its creation, Policy Governance® has been recognized universally as a sound model based on inarguable theory. It offers a logical process for boards to govern well, and to remove themselves from the day-to-day operational matters that too frequently consume board members' time and attention. At the same time, the model allows the board to control, through policy, the extent of authority delegated to the CEO and staff, and to monitor actual organizational performance to assure complete accountability.

COHERENT GOVERNANCE

Coherent Governance® is our own governance design, influenced by John Carver's work. It is a variation of Policy Governance®, resulting from our own work with clients whose actual needs seemed to require more than modest changes to existing models.

In particular, the modifications are geared to meet the specific conditions that exist in many public and nonprofit organizations, especially in the field of public education and other such environments with elected board members. The changes are intended to address the full range of operational issues and concerns such boards face.

The Coherent Governance® model is built around four different but interrelated types of policies, each serving a very distinct purpose:

Results: Results policies describe the outcomes the organization is expected to achieve for the specific clients or customers it serves. Results policies are the performance targets for the CEO and the organization, and form the basis for judging the success of both.

Operational Expectations: Most boards want to remove themselves from preoccupation with the day-to-day operation of the organization. Yet they have concerns about those operational matters that they must express in order to represent and serve the interests of the board's "owners," those on whose behalf the board does its work.

OE policies allow the board either to direct that certain conditions exist or actions occur, or to prohibit those conditions and actions the board would find unacceptable. Each OE policy is clearly and unambiguously stated, and has two components: one stated positively ("do this"), the other negatively ("don't do this").

The CEO is encumbered to comply with the board's stated values about operational conditions and actions. OE policies allow the board to control operational decisions without the confusing ritual of approving CEO recommendations that undermines clear accountability.

The Coherent Governance board rigorously monitors organizational compliance with its Operational Expectations policies and reasonable progress toward the achievement of its Results policies.

Board-CEO Relations: BCR policies define the degree of authority conveyed by the board to the CEO, and also outline the process for CEO evaluation. Essentially, the performance of the CEO and the performance of the organization are the same: if the organization succeeds in operating according to the board's stated values, and if it produces the outcomes specified by the board in policy, the CEO has succeeded and is evaluated accordingly.

Governance Culture: All boards have cultures. In traditional governing environments, we aren't quite sure what causes them to be what they are. In the Coherent Governance model, the board deliberately and carefully crafts a set of policies that, in sum, establishes a culture for good governance. Separate policies establish standards for how the board performs its work, including policies that define the board's job, its purpose, and its accountability.

Both Coherent Governance® and Policy Governance® establish standards of performance for everything, from the boardroom to the boiler room. The Governance Culture/Governance Process policies set the standards for the board's own performance. The Board-CEO Relationship/Governance-Management Connection policies set standards for how the board will interact with the CEO, defining what organizational success is and how it will be monitored.

The Operational Expectations/Executive Limitations policies establish operational standards for the entire organization. The Results/Ends policies define the standard for organizational outcomes, specifically the value promised to those served by the organization.

In sum, then, both Coherent Governance® and Policy Governance® are complete systems enabling governing boards to do their work in a logical way that drives organizational response and alignment. Both models require commitment and discipline by the board, support and serious attention by the CEO and staff, and patience by all while new skills are learned and new processes developed.

The remainder of this book is focused on the specific strategies that boards and CEOs should consider as the model is implemented, beginning with initial steps to announce the board's new way of doing business, then progressing through all the essential components of effective implementation. Chapter 2 begins that journey with suggestions for rolling out the model to owners and both internal and external groups that have an interest in the work of the board.

Chapter 2

Rolling Out Your Model

You have done something important. You have:

- Made a commitment to forge stronger relationships with the owners you represent and serve, seeking to assure that their desired results for the clients served by your organization are reflected in your Results policies;
- Made a commitment to elevate your focus to allow the board to spend the bulk of its time dealing with what really matters: the benefits your clients are entitled to receive as a result of your efforts;
- Agreed to hold your CEO—and therefore the entire staff—accountable for achieving Results;
- Established clear performance expectations for your CEO, with regular monitoring processes built in; and
- Committed to govern the organization from the *policy* level with great discipline.

Now, how and when do you present this new focus and these commitments to the people who need to know? How can you build understanding of and support for this bold new venture? How do you explain to key staff how this adoption of a new governing model will affect them and their jobs?

GETTING STARTED

This is our best advice, with some exceptions we will discuss later: Simply adopt the policies and start your journey. Begin your new work, allowing your internal operating processes and the texture of your board meetings themselves to gradually educate those who need to know what you have done, at least those outside the organization. People assume that the board has some means for doing its work, so usually there is little need for them to understand the intricacies of what those processes are. For people inside the organization, that may not always be the case, as we will discuss later.

Start the process by taking action to adopt the policies with a formal motion, similar to the following:

> Over the past ___ months, the board deliberatively and thoughtfully has created a new set of governing policies that will allow us to lead this organization in a much more powerful and accountable way. All members have participated in this venture. We have refined our values-driven policies to the point that we are ready to adopt and begin this exciting journey toward aligned and improved organizational performance, beginning in the boardroom and extending to every worksite.
>
> Therefore, Mr./Madam President, I move that the board adopt our completed set of governing policies, and appropriately refer all of our current operational policies to the CEO for his/her use in the day-to-day operation of the organization.

Notice that the motion has two significant parts:

- *Part 1* asks the board to adopt its new policies.
- *Part 2* refers all current policies to the CEO. This is important, especially if yours is a public board, because many or most of your old policies likely are based on some state or federal mandate; they must be retained in some fashion. We recommend renaming them "Operational Policies" and making them the property of the CEO. They should retain the "policy" designation, since in many instances they are policies required by some superior authority.

By being designated "Operational Policies," they clearly are separated from the board's new "Governing Policies" and now are the responsibility of the CEO for the routine operation of the organization. It is at the CEO's level of operations that they have the most import anyway. Most of them are much too detailed and prescriptive for effective governance use.

Some may question whether the board is taking an undue risk by referring its old policies to the CEO. *It is not.* OE-1 requires the CEO to comply with law, and thus the CEO has no discretion to circumvent any current or future provisions of those policies that are legally required.

After the board's approval of its new policies, let's consider some rollout strategies to position the board for success.

HITTING THE MARK . . . WITHOUT CREATING A TARGET

We prefer and recommend a very low-key strategy to begin the board's work using the new governance system. However, if the board feels compelled to make some public announcement about the new system, we strongly encourage the board to completely avoid the use of a label. Labeling your efforts can create a highly convenient target. When your owners, stakeholders, and staff think they have another new trend to survive, it will be easy for them to take potshots at everything. And if a visible label is attached (Coherent Governance®), sooner or later it will become "the reason" for whatever future problems the organization encounters.

Instead, focus on the board's commitment to realign its own performance. Something like the following may be a reasonable statement to make:

> The board has allowed itself to become overly involved in issues related to day-to-day operations that have prevented it from focusing on organizational results. Members have committed to elevate our primary focus to the results the organization should achieve for the people we serve, and to remove ourselves from preoccupation with routine management operations. The board has adopted a new set of governing policies to enable it to better lead this organization. The CEO will be allowed to execute his/her job without interference from the board, but with rigorous accountability and regular reporting of organizational performance and compliance with the board's policies.

Notice that the label "Coherent Governance" or "Policy Governance" is never used. The board has adopted new *governance policies*. Avoidance of labels is a good practice to observe.

Never fail to underscore this emphasis on clear accountability for delegated decisions. People who do not understand the governing model may choose to criticize the board for having given too much authority to the CEO. Such assumptions are completely false, of course, but people, especially those who do not understand the offsetting accountability, tend to focus more on delegation than on accountability.

Another explanation of your enhanced board role that may apply (this is for a school board, but is modifiable) could sound like this:

> We have heard from our owners and our stakeholders that performance in our organization must improve. To model and lead that improvement, we as a board are committed to our own self-improvement through a dedicated focus on organizational success. In the future, our meetings and discussion will center on that topic. We actively will engage all segments of our community in this ongoing

challenge by providing an instructional program to assure that our students meet or exceed the highest and most rigorous standards.

Big statements. Big commitment. But now is not a time to present an image that you are doing something radical that causes a backlash of concern. You are simply going to do the job you were elected or appointed to do: operate as a board exercising prudence and wisdom through your simple, clear policies to set the direction for your organization. And you are going to release the CEO and staff to do their jobs, and yet hold them responsible for making Results happen.

INFORMING STAFF

Staff members, at least at the senior level, must be brought into the loop. After all, if the board's new vision for the organization never leaves the boardroom, not much will change within the organization. Alignment from the boardroom throughout the operational side of the organization is necessary for anything meaningful to occur. That cannot happen without key staff members understanding and supporting the operational changes that will be driven by the board's work and their role in the evolution.

Staff members likely will know that the board has been working on new policies and a new governance process. For them, there is a "FUD" factor (*Fear, Uncertainty, and Doubt*) at work. What happens to them? How will this new board focus change their lives? Their position could swing negatively against accepting and supporting the board's new venture, unless deliberate steps are taken to assure full understanding of what the board has done and why it did it.

The question is, who should bring staff members into the loop? The governing model provides that all staff members report to the CEO, and the CEO is the board's only employee. Does this mean that the board cannot interface with any staff to explain the model and the important role the board depends on staff to play in advancing the organization?

Strict interpretation of the model could suggest that to be the case. However, common sense must come into play here. The culture, size, and complexity of the organization itself must be considered. The only hard-and-fast rule we recommend is that the board and the CEO jointly decide how much board face time might be constructive in presenting this new venture to staff and how much of that burden the CEO wants to assume without the board's involvement.

We have worked with organizations in which the task was accomplished quite effectively with the board playing no role. In others, the CEO chose to invite the board to interface directly with senior staff for extensive give-and-take, and this too worked very well. We emphasize that if the board and CEO agree that there is a constructive role for the board to play in informing staff, the task for the board is to *inform,* not to direct, the work of staff.

However the work is organized, we recommend that the void be filled fast with information and positive statements. The CEO should determine quickly when, where, and how to assure that top administrative staff fully understand all they need to know about the board's governing work and how the work of staff may be affected.

If the board meets with senior administrative staff members directly, it should emphasize that the board respects their professionalism, experience, and expertise, *and that the board recognizes its job to be different from theirs.* The model releases them to do their work, with the board's support, as it aligns with the board's expectations for Results and for operational decision-making.

Senior administrative staff members must grasp the concept that this is organization-wide and strategic alignment initiated and modeled by the governing board. The board will direct and evaluate only the CEO, and only through policy. In turn, all staff members will be directed and evaluated by the CEO based upon their contribution to achieving reasonable progress on Results and their faithful compliance with the operational policies.

A caution: Staff must have full and accurate information about what the board is doing, without the "reform of the month" flavor. Effective implementation of systems and processes can take years to fully achieve. Staff will need to understand that they will not outlive the board's commitment to move the organization in a new direction.

If the board meets with staff below the senior administration level, it should be with the understanding that the purpose is to assure full knowledge of what the board has done and how it will affect them, and *not* to build direct relationships around the CEO. Any such meetings should be acceptable to the CEO, who should be a part of the discussions.

STAFF AS AMBASSADORS

Staff members are known to be credible, go-to sources for information about the organization. Indeed, research tells us that the owners find the staff more credible than board members or the CEO! In schools, parents accept their child's teacher's opinion before the opinions of all others. Families of elders in support care find their parents to be the first line of information.

Below are examples of how two clients chose to assure initial staff understanding of the board's work.

EXAMPLE A

Nikkei Concerns is a nonprofit, community-based elder care system serving the Japanese American community in Seattle, Washington. The board and CEO recognized that staff members, who also are intimately tied to the small and closely knit community, would be opinion leaders for family members, clients, and community members who would begin to see a change and wonder how this work was benefiting the organization's elder clients.

The rollout for Nikkei Concerns became a three-step process. First, before work began with the board, at the request of the board and CEO, we met with senior staff to assure that they understood where the project would lead in terms of board focus and how it ultimately would affect staff work.

Second, once the policies were adopted and the board agendas and other board work began to change, we met with all senior staff members for a second overview of Coherent Governance® and to respond to any questions or concerns they might have based on the specific policy product the board had produced.

Finally, we conducted a meeting between senior staff and board for the purpose of building a stronger bridge of mutual understanding and a relationship that would serve them as they work together to meet their owners' and clients' needs. The board wanted to have an honest give-and-take session with staff about their concerns and hopes.

EXAMPLE B

Years ago, we directed a Policy Governance® project with a school board in Texas. The superintendent at that time, along with his staff, was challenged to assure that his staff of more than 11,000 employees, including 450 administrators at 120 school sites, understood the board's new emphasis and how it would affect their jobs. It was a Herculean task that called for a plan for systemic communication and commitment.

We share with you the following two documents that serve as a record of the superintendent's approach to presenting the board's work to internal staff at all levels. This effort assured that all staff members knew what this new venture was before the board began a series of linkages throughout the community to build support for the Results.

Office of the CEO

ACTION REQUIRED

Memorandum
To: Principals
From: CEO

Subject: Professional Development Regarding Policy Governance®

Date: November 7

As part of the district's transition to Policy Governance, we need to conduct an awareness initiative over the next three months.

It is my expectation that you will share this information with your campus staff, CACs, and PTAs. We will ask for verification when each campus has met with these groups. How and when you conduct the training is a local campus decision. However, I expect all phases of the training to be completed by February 2.

The School Board adopted a new model of governance during the summer and reaffirmed its commitment on September 15. This new model is referred to as "Policy Governance."

In the year and a half we have been working toward full implementation, I have come to appreciate the power and usefulness of this approach to defining what is "board work" and what is "staff work." Although most groups that work in the area of board governance stress the need to know the difference between setting policy and administering policy, they do not have the comprehensiveness and specificity of Policy Governance.

Until now, we have not spent a lot of time on the intricacies of Policy Governance. However, I do hope the board's RESULTS policies are familiar to you.

The board has set the expectation that our stakeholders—both staff and patrons—have an exposure to this model. To facilitate this awareness effort we have attached for your use three documents (which will also be provided electronically) that track with three phases of training (which can be accomplished within one to three sessions):

- *Phase One Training*—a Q&A brochure (in English and Spanish) that summarizes the information found on the website. (Sufficient copies will be sent to your campus via school mail by the end of next week.)

- *Phase Two Training*—a PowerPoint presentation that goes into a little more detail about Policy Governance.
- *Phase Three Training*—a second PowerPoint that outlines the Executive Limitation policies most relevant to district staff members.

The Associate CEOs will be working more closely with you in the very near future to more fully explain the training materials and the specific training objectives and can help answer any questions.

I thank you, in advance, for your help in this matter.

Questions

Policy Governance Awareness Initiative

Campus Verification

Your assistance in this matter is most appreciated!

School:
Principal's Signature:

My signature above serves as documentation that my campus has completed the three phases of the Policy Governance awareness initiative with the following groups:

1. Campus Staff:	(Date)
2. Campus Advisory Council:	(Date)
3. PTA:	(Date)

Please email or send via school mail this complete and signed form to your Associate CEO prior to February 2.

Questions for Thought

1. Has your board considered whether it is advisable to communicate with any stakeholder groups about your new governing system?
2. How will you and/or your CEO communicate to your key administrative staff members the importance of this new governing system and build a relationship that has at its root a common focus on Results?
3. Who in your organizational framework are key opinion leaders who can help build support for your new venture?

FAQs

Q: Should we involve senior staff with the board as the policies are developed, rather than educating them later? If we don't do that, how do we get their buy-in after the fact?

A: The choice of who should be in the room when the policies are developed should be made jointly by the board and CEO. We tend to believe it is helpful to the board for key administrative staff to be available as technical advisors as the OE and Results policies are developed, to be called upon as needed. If they are involved from the start, less after-the-fact education will be necessary.

Q: If we decide to present our new governance work to stakeholders, should we start with "inside" groups or "outside" groups?

A: There really is no right answer, because every organization may have circumstances that make it logical to start in one place or the other. However, as a rule, we recommend starting with staff and other inside groups, since they can help sell your ideas to outside groups and because their jobs will be affected by your venture.

Q: What do we do if some important people and groups resist our new governing model?

A: Good up-front strategy about the message and how to present it can help minimize the likelihood of that, but if it happens, the board must be resolute in its commitment to forge ahead. Your ultimate success will be the best method of deflecting any opposition. If people or groups resist, back away and assess their reasons. Are those reasons valid, or are they based on misunderstanding? Is their resistance grounded in their fear of losing something? Are there things the board can do to help them overcome their fears or misunderstandings?

Chapter 3

Monitoring Governance Culture and Board-CEO Relations Policies

The board has identified in its Governance Culture policies its values about how it should do its work, and in its Board-CEO Relationship policies how it will interact with its CEO. These policies actually are operational standards for board behavior. As such, they provide a logical basis for the board to effectively monitor its own performance.

In order for the board to remain faithful to those policies and the performance standards they represent, the board has committed to regularly monitor its performance against those policy standards. Faithful and rigorous self-monitoring of these policies allows the board to:

- Compare its actions with its policy values to determine whether it has performed as it committed to perform;
- Provide a means for self-correction if actions deviate from policy;
- Maintain clarity of roles; and
- Model continuing performance improvement, as well as build capacity for sustainability in the event of board or CEO turnover.

There is no single way to monitor board performance in the Governance Culture and Board-CEO Relations areas. The important thing is to do it!

We have found that it is difficult for public boards to effectively self-monitor during a public business meeting, in front of an audience, and often with the cameras rolling. To compound the problem, laws requiring open meetings generally prevent public boards from doing such work in closed sessions.

Options include work sessions, which, although technically "open," usually are not covered by news media or attended by members of the public. Some boards hold pre-meeting work sessions, which also are technically open, but yet usually enable more free-flowing conversation.

Regardless of the environment in which boards choose to conduct self-assessments, there are a variety of processes we have found to be successful. Some require members to record their individual conclusions about board compliance in advance, while others require nothing prior to the board's discussion. We discuss below some of the strategies that various boards have used, without recommendation of a specific one. Readers will find one, or create their own variation, that seems appropriate for them.

EXAMPLE A

Some boards self-monitor by dividing the GC and BCR policies into increments coinciding with the number of meetings the board holds each year, and monitor one or two policies at each meeting. Exhibit 3.1 illustrates how one board collects individual member feedback via a written form prior to the meeting, synthesizes individual responses into one document, and presents it to the whole board at the meeting for discussion and action.

EXHIBIT 3.1

GC MONITORING REPORT

GC-7 Annual Board Planning Cycle

To: Board of Trustees
From: Governance Committee
Date:

GC-7 Global Policy Statement

To accomplish its work with a governance style consistent with board policies, the board will follow an annual agenda which (a) completes a review of Results policies at least bi-annually, (b) improves its performance through attention to board education and enriched input and deliberation, and (c) completes the monitoring of Operational Expectations policies, Governance Culture policies, and Board-CEO Relationship policies.

GC-7 Policy Subparts

1. The cycle will conclude each year on the last day of March in order that administrative decisions and budgeting can be based on accomplishing the current board policies.

   In compliance. This year's monitoring cycle begins with our April 8 meeting and will end with the last meeting in March.
2. In the first two months of the new cycle, the board will develop its agenda for the ensuing one-year period.

   In compliance. The board will schedule on its agenda for the first meeting in May action to adopt the new annual board calendar for the coming year.
3. Education, input, and deliberation will receive paramount attention in structuring board meetings and other board activities during the year.

   Not in compliance. The board has received its first Results monitoring reports in three areas. There has been considerable effort made to allow for the majority of time to be spent evaluating and discussing these reports.

   However, there have been two issues this year that have been in front of the board for an excessive amount time and have taken away from the board's priority function, to address Results for our clients.

Commitment to Improve

As a result of the excess time spent on these issues, the board will look at its procedure for having items on its agenda for reconsideration. The board did reconstruct its form for "Audience Comments" in an effort to be more efficient when it receives input from the community.

Approved: Date:

Exhibit 3.1 is the result of the board's discussion and group action after these individual forms were compiled and discussed. The board uses a Governance Committee, which recorded the board's action and prepared this summary for the full board. Note that the board has identified why it is noncompliant and what it will do to improve its performance.

To reiterate, we do not recommend that public boards try to self-monitor during a public meeting. If the example cited here is used, discussion and action should be done in some type of session other than a public business meeting.

EXAMPLE B

Many boards conduct full self-assessments of all GC and BCR policies at an annual retreat. This self-assessment usually serves as a precursor to the CEO evaluation and establishment of the board's annual priorities and calendar. It is logical to conduct the board's self-assessment in conjunction with the CEO evaluation, since the board and CEO are so intimately linked through these policies. It also signifies to the CEO that the board is willing to review its own performance as it reviews the CEO's.

For both GC and BCR policies, one of the most efficient processes we have seen is a highly visual, no-homework, no-paperwork process. Using such a method allows the board to monitor all GC and BCR policies at one time at an annual retreat, or the process can be done in increments at quarterly mini-retreats.

The process: Prior to the meeting during which the self-assessment occurs, the board's policies are enlarged to fit flip chart–size paper. We suggest laminating the pages and mounting them on core board for more permanent use. During the meeting, board members are provided a set of colored sticky dots, and each member is asked to place a sticky dot to identify those policies or subsections that the member perceives to be out of compliance. The resulting visual quickly "tees up" those areas that need discussion and action to improve board performance.

The full board discusses the areas that are identified as noncompliant, deciding as a majority whether the board's performance has met expectations and what corrective actions are necessary. We recommend that the CEO be included in the process.

Exhibit 3.2 is an illustration of this method. Note that the default choice is "compliant"; dots are placed only where members believe the board has failed to meet the standards it set for itself. These noncompliant provisions of policy become the basis for board discussion and commitment to corrective action.

EXHIBIT 3.2

GC MONITORING: VISUAL WITH ENTIRE BOARD

GC-7

Annual Agenda Planning

To accomplish its stated objectives, the board will follow an annual agenda that schedules continuing review, monitoring, and refinement of *Results* policies; linkage meetings with community, student, and staff groups; monitoring of policies; and activities to improve board performance through education, enriched input, and deliberation.

COMPLIANT	**NONCOMPLIANT**

Accordingly:

1. The planning cycle will end each year in January in order that administrative decision-making and budgeting for the forthcoming year can begin and be based on accomplishing the next one-year segment of the board's most recent statement of long-term *Results*.

2. The planning cycle will start with the board's development of its annual agenda for the next year, and will include:
   a. Scheduled dialog discussions and consultations with selected groups and persons whose insights and opinions will be helpful to the board;

   b. Discussions on governance matters, including orientation of new board members in the board's governance process, and periodic discussions by the board about means to improve its own performance;

   c. Education related to *Results* policies (e.g., presentations by futurists, demographers, advocacy groups, staff, etc.);

d. Scheduled monitoring of all policies.

3. The board will take action to update the Agenda Planning Calendar as necessary. A copy of the calendar is placed in the board folders at every regularly scheduled meeting.

4. Throughout the year the board will attend to consent agenda items as expeditiously as possible. An item may be removed from the consent agenda only upon approval of a majority of the board.

5. Monitoring of *Operational Expectations* policies that were previously accepted by the board as having been in full compliance will be included on the agenda for separate discussion only if the report indicates superintendent noncompliance, if a majority of the board has questions about superintendent compliance or reasonable interpretation, or if policy content is to be debated. Otherwise *OE* monitoring reports will be included in the consent agenda.

ALTERNATIVES TO SELF-ASSESSMENT

Effectively assessing one's own performance can be difficult, even it the board enjoys the luxury of doing it in closed session. There are options, if the board has interest in looking at them.

One option is to hire an outside consultant to observe the board in action, examine its processes and documents, interview members and the CEO, and render a third-party assessment based on the findings. This isn't foolproof, however, because sometimes the issues the board itself understands are not apparent to such third parties. Not all performance issues are apparent during formal meetings, nor are they necessarily revealed in the documents compiled by the board.

Nevertheless, this is an option that the board might consider in certain circumstances. If the board is primarily concerned, for example, with meeting efficiency or the proper use of parliamentary procedure, it may be appropriate to consider the use of a consultant to assess what is happening and offer recommendations for improvement. This option may not be viable if the board is struggling with interpersonal issues that may not be observable during a brief interaction with the board and its members.

A few years ago, a client board decided to create a committee of the board to observe each of its meetings and offer appropriate feedback afterward. This "External Monitoring Committee" was comprised of twelve members, representing various elements of the stakeholders; it even included some staff members.

We met with the committee after its creation to explain in detail how the board governed and reviewed very carefully the relevant policies that deal with board and board member expectations. These policies were the standards the committee used to critique the board's performance during meetings. The committee then divided itself into two subcommittees of six persons each. The subcommittees alternated attendance at the meetings.

After each meeting, the subcommittee chair drafted a brief report to the board highlighting the areas of the board's performance the committee felt warranted commendation and those that deserved some attention. Once each quarter, the full committee met with the board for a face-to-face discussion of the highlights and lowlights of the board's work during the previous quarter, as observed by the committee.

This process worked quite well for the board, but there were reasons for that. Members of the committee were appointed because of their integrity and their perceived ability to offer constructive criticism, to be neither full-time critics of—nor cheerleaders for—the board. Members were thoroughly trained about and knowledgeable of the board's governing system, and fully prepared to intelligently look for the things that worked and those that did not. And the members were dedicated to the task, which involved substantial amounts of their own time. One report of the committee is shared as a sample in chapter 9.

IN SUMMARY

These options all are worthy of consideration, but the board very likely will decide that self-assessment of its performance is the preferred way to go about measuring actual performance against the standards set in policy.

As we stated at the beginning of this chapter, there are many ways to self-assess performance against the board's own standards. Boards tend to fare better in self-assessment exercises if they use a third-party facilitator who understands the board's processes and performance standards and who can help manage any personality clashes or interpersonal conflicts that might arise. We emphasize that if a facilitator is used, the person needs to be fully attuned to the governance system the board is using and prepared to offer recommendations appropriate for the system.

What must not be allowed to happen is failure to self-assess. We have heard these excuses for not doing it: *too little time; no one will take it seriously; it's uncomfortable; we might create rifts; we have more important issues to deal with.*

Nevertheless, the board committed to govern with excellence. Now it must exercise the required maturity and personal discipline to evaluate its performance over time, diagnose problems, and commit to actions for continuous improvement. The board should be just as diligent in assessing its own performance as it is in assessing the performance of the CEO and the organization. Doing so demonstrates the same degree of accountability the board expects from the organization.

Questions for Thought

1. Why is it important for the board to continuously assess its own performance?
2. What is the standard against which the board assesses its performance?
3. What does the board do when its performance fails to meet the standards it set for itself?

FAQs

Q: Should senior administrative staff be involved in the board's self-assessment?

A: The presence and participation of other staff may not allow for full and open communication among members. However, as a rule, we believe the CEO should participate.

Q: What is the best timing on the annual work plan for a board self-evaluation?

A: If all GC and BCR policies are monitored at the same time, it is our experience that the exercise is best done in a board retreat in conjunction with the CEO's summative evaluation. If monitoring is spread throughout the year, the board should determine the intervals and sequence that make sense to the members.

Q: Should any voting on compliance by individual members be anonymous, or should each member's identity be known?

A: If individuals feel they can't or won't acknowledge their opinions and explain why they voted as they did, it is difficult to have a meaningful conversation that diagnoses problems and activates self-improvement. Therefore, we suggest that all members openly share their opinions with other members of the board.

Chapter 4

Monitoring Operational Expectations Policies

On behalf of the community of owners the board serves, it has worked hard to identify the values within which the CEO, and therefore all staff, must make all operational decisions. These Operational Expectations policies define the degree of authority transferred to the CEO and staff as they make day-to-day decisions.

Operational Expectations policies constitute the board's standards for the organization's operational performance. The staff is required by policy to:

1. *Reasonably interpret* the board's policy language;
2. *Operate in compliance* with the policies' values.

The purpose of Operational Expectations monitoring, stated simply, is to assure the board that the CEO and staff reasonably understand the values underlying the board's policies, and that the organization is operating in a compliant manner.

Monitoring OE policies is one of the board's most important functions, one to which it committed in its job description.

The board has delegated substantial authority to the CEO to do his or her job without board interference or approvals. The trade-off is for the board to gain solid evidence that the CEO's actions and decisions, and those made by any part of the organization, are within the parameters of the policies.

This commitment to rigorous monitoring does not mean that every OE monitoring event is an opportunity to cross-examine the CEO or to dig deeply into the operations of the organization to "see what's going on." Some might say that the monitoring process, if abused, is an opportunity for the board to "legally" micromanage the organization.

If the board is using the process to catch the CEO doing something wrong, or if it finds itself so focused on operational monitoring that it compromises its commitment to place Results at the top of the list in importance, the system is being abused.

But the other side of this coin is equally important: monitoring OE performance should not be a rote action, void of meaning and rigor. Some boards are inclined to trust their CEO to do the right thing, and accept compliance as a default position.

That isn't good enough. Having trust in the CEO is a good thing, far better than not having trust. *But this system of governance is not dependent on trust.* Even if the board has complete confidence and trust in its CEO, it is not doing its job if it fails to demand convincing evidence of organizational performance. Some boards appropriately look at the monitoring process as one built on a theme of "trust, but verify."

The board can delegate any degree of authority to the CEO it chooses, but that delegation must be accompanied by solid documentation from the CEO that the interpretation of the board's policy is reasonable and that compliance has been achieved.

WHAT CONSTITUTES EFFECTIVE MONITORING?

Monitoring compliance is a formal, planned process, not a random or rote act. Effectively performing this responsibility:

- Assures the board that organizational performance is in compliance with the board's values, as expressed in OE policy;
- Allows the board to delegate with assurance that it will know the true operational condition of the organization;
- Provides important information to the board about the operational organization and arms the board for its support and advocacy roles;
- Builds one-half of the CEO's annual performance portfolio.

Effective OE monitoring should be viewed as a very positive exercise intended not only to accomplish the objectives listed above, but also to build communication between the board and CEO about the true operational condition of the organization. Since OE monitoring comprises half of the CEO's annual performance evaluation, it should be viewed as a serious obligation to be well executed by both the board and the CEO.

The basic purpose of OE monitoring, again, is to satisfy the board that its policy values are clearly and reasonably understood and are being complied with. Reports should provide ample information for that judgment to be made. If they do not, they should be done again with a reasonable interpretation and information sufficient to allow the board to reach that conclusion.

Monitoring information must be sufficient for the board to make an informed decision, but it need not be exhaustive. Initially, a round or two of reporting and responding may be necessary to establish the amount, type, and quality of information required to satisfy the board.

All good OE monitoring reports contain certain required elements in order for the board to make an informed judgment of organizational performance. These elements include a restatement of the board's policy, section by section. Each section is followed by:

- The CEO's literal interpretation of the board's policy provision;
- Identified, quantifiable "indicators" the CEO will use to judge compliance;
- A statement of organizational condition with regard to that specific policy provision—either in compliance or out of compliance;
- Evidence of that condition, using data from the indicators;
- If out of compliance, an explanation of the reasons for that condition, information about what is being done to gain compliance and the projected date for compliance to be achieved.

WHY ALL THE FUSS ABOUT INTERPRETATION AND INDICATORS?

Interpretation of the board's policy language may be the most important part of a good monitoring report. This is why: people don't respond to the words we use; they respond to *their interpretation* of the words we use. The board must be assured that the very broad language it used in its policies is reasonably interpreted. That interpretation drives not only the organization's actions, but also the CEO's choice of indicators and the body of compliance data.

An example: In several places in most board policy manuals, the value of "safety" is stated. The board wants working conditions to be safe. What does that term mean? Does it mean that no individual ever will be injured at any time under any circumstances? If so, no organization ever could be compliant.

If that interpretation is not reasonable, what are the alternatives? What is a reasonable interpretation of that value that allows the organization to achieve compliance? How "safe" does a workplace need to be before it is compliant? Or how "unsafe" must it be before it is noncompliant?

Ultimately, the CEO is obligated to report to the board that the organization either is compliant or noncompliant with the stated value of "safe." How will that judgment be made?

It depends upon how "safe" is interpreted, and the indicators that have been selected to measure whether actual conditions are safe. It all revolves around the interpretation of the board's value, and whether the board and CEO are in agreement with the reasonable standard of interpretation.

LITERAL INTERPRETATION OF THE BOARD'S LANGUAGE

Let's look at each part of this interpretation component separately, beginning with the literal interpretation. In developing an interpretation, the staff *never* should use the same words the board used in its policy. Simply restating the same words fails to tell the board if staff understand the underlying value of the policy. The board deserves to know what "safe" means to the CEO as the staff apply that value to operational conditions.

The CEO might respond in a monitoring report by applying the following interpretation to the term: "I interpret 'safe' to mean '*secure from physical, emotional, or psychological danger or harm.*'" This interpretation could be extended to specify the physical and operational areas included in the application of the word, such as "*at all buildings and sites and all off-site activities for which the organization is responsible*," for example.

This interpretation does not guarantee that no one will ever be injured at a site or during an activity under the control of the organization. But if many people are being injured on property owned by the organization, one might conclude that conditions are noncompliant.

If that is the case, just how many people can be injured before the organization becomes noncompliant? And what kinds of injury, under what circumstances, should be factored into the equation? Remember, perfection is not the standard; the standard is *reasonable.*

INTERPRETATIONS THAT DRIVE SELECTION OF INDICATORS

That is why the second part of the interpretation becomes so important. What indicators will the staff use to judge whether the organization is in compliance with the board's value of safety? What is a reasonable performance standard?

We encourage the staff to use the following process to make that call: "*We will know we are compliant when . . .*"

The sentence may be completed by such options as the following: "*When the number of workers' compensation claims filed by employees during the year is five or fewer.*" Or, "*When the number of students sustaining serious injury on school property during the year is two or fewer at any school site.*" Or, "*When fire department inspections reveal zero major violations and two or fewer minor exceptions to the fire code at all school sites during the year.*"

Your board may not like some of these indicators, but the important thing to note is that all are very precise and quantifiable.

If the board has accepted the choice of indicators as a part of the CEO's interpretation, and if internal processes reveal that the performance targets were realized, then the organization is, by definition, compliant.

If the numbers were not realized, the organization is noncompliant, and improvement is needed. Unless there are some justifiable aberrations to be considered, there should be no debate about the condition of the organization, either by the board or by the staff.

The board always has the final decision about whether such an interpretation is reasonable. But it is important to remember the standard for interpretation the board stated in policy; it is *reasonable.*

The board did not say that it would approve only interpretations that it considers "perfect," or those that meet the personal preferences of individual members. There are many ways to interpret "safe," and the number of potential indicators is large.

The *reasonable* standard must be applied each time the judgment is made, or the board is back in the micromanagement business.

If the CEO presents to the board an interpretation or proposed indicators that the board or some of its members consider unreasonable, the temptation will be to substitute the board's choices for those of the CEO.

Avoid that at all costs. Amending a CEO report to substitute the board's preferences means that the board is doing the CEO's work, and therefore accountability is transferred back to the board. Remember the principle "S/he who makes a decision is accountable for the result."

Instead, if a report is considered unreasonable, the board should not accept it, and should allow the CEO and staff another opportunity to submit a report that is reasonable. One would hope that such a process is rarely required. But returning a report is far better than the board's substituting its decisions for those that belong to the CEO.

The example in exhibit 4.1 is a partial OE monitoring report that includes both an interpretation and indicators. This example does not include actual monitoring data. It reflects the first step in a two-step monitoring sequence, which we discuss in more detail below. The format of this report is one we recommend; it is simple, clear, and concise.

EXHIBIT 4.1

Sample Interpretation and Indicators Report

OE 3: Learning Environment/ Treatment of Students/Discipline	Interpretation		Indicators	
The superintendent shall establish and maintain a learning environment that is safe, disciplined, respectful, and conducive to effective learning.	Reasonable	Not Reasonable	Reasonable	Not Reasonable

Reasonable Interpretation

- The district will provide a positive educational atmosphere wherever learning occurs (i.e., classrooms, ball fields, performance stages, technology labs, field trips, etc.).
- A safe learning environment is structured and secure so that student health (physical, social-emotional) is not compromised, and students are protected from harm on school campuses or other educational settings.
- A disciplined learning environment is safe and orderly and adheres to a discipline plan that is communicated to all stakeholders and consistently applied.
- A respectful learning environment is one where:
  - Mutual consideration exists among all stakeholders.
  - Rules and student rights are clearly communicated and equitably applied.
  - Curricular and extracurricular opportunities are made known and are equitably available to all students.
  - Differing opinions are welcomed.
- An environment that is conducive to effective learning is one that:
  - Is clean and well maintained.
  - Has textbooks and instructional materials that are readily available.
  - Has minimal disruptions.
  - Has rigorous and engaging instruction.
  - Includes teachers who demonstrate effective classroom management techniques and who have knowledge of content they are teaching.

Indicators of Compliance

- School sites are allocated sufficient personnel to maintain cleanliness and supervise the campus per district maintenance and safety standards.
- Facilities personnel monitor and prioritize school site work orders to ensure timeliness in responding to maintenance requests.
- A clearly defined, widely communicated discipline plan is collaboratively created and implemented at each school site.
- Annual site climate survey results are analyzed to assess effectiveness of learning environments and to inform modifications.
- Annual Williams inspection reports include standards for cleanliness, safety, and maintenance and document that sites are free of safety hazards.
- Annual Williams inspection reports verify that textbooks and instructional materials are available to all students.

Evidence of Compliance: *(to be completed when the monitoring report is finalized)*

Data and analysis inserted here

Process: *(additional information re: operational strategies and actions)*

Capacity Building: *(resources, timeframe, cost to achieve full compliance or improve)*

OE MONITORING PROCESS

When the board is first launching its practice of Coherent Governance®, we recommend a two-step process for monitoring OE policies. This is why: if the CEO's interpretation, including the choice of indicators, is not considered reasonable by the board, there is a good chance that when monitoring data are presented, the report will be unacceptable to the board.

As a first step, we believe it is preferable to have the board and CEO establish common understanding about the reasonable interpretation and compliance indicators that will be used. It is at the second step, which comes later, that the CEO presents actual monitoring data aligned with the interpretation and chosen indicators.

Step 1

In the first step of this two-step monitoring process, the CEO presents only a reasonable interpretation of the policy and each of its sub-parts, along with compliance indicators. These indicators are intended to be the observable conditions that the staff plan to use to judge whether the organization is compliant.

The board should approve the interpretation and indicators. This action assures the CEO that when compliance information is presented later, that information will be based upon an interpretation and indicators that already have been accepted by the board as reasonable.

Step 2

In the second step, the CEO finalizes the report by presenting compliance data based upon the board's previously approved interpretation and indicators. Since the data are based on the indicators and the selected performance targets, this final piece should be the simplest and least debatable part of the process.

There should be a reasonable time interval between the first and second steps in order for the staff to effectively assess the organization's actual condition and to compile documentation for the compliance report.

Although this two-step sequence may slow the implementation process a bit during the first year, the delay should not be a major factor in the long run. This sequence applies only to the first monitoring cycle, since the interpretation is unlikely to change appreciably from one cycle to the other. Performance targets should be adjusted based on actual performance.

The second and subsequent monitoring cycles can omit the first step, and proceed as a single event that includes all components.

Board Action

Regardless of the process—either two-step or one-step—once the report is presented, the board should formally act on it through a vote. Board action should result in one of the following choices:

- *Compliance*
- *Not in compliance*
- *Compliance, with noted exception(s)*

The board's vote is recorded on the monitoring report cover, along with any amending motions (such as action to commend), in order to serve as a record and to inform board discussion during the CEO's summative evaluation.

This action closes the loop on that particular monitoring event. The monitoring document and board summary cover become a part of the CEO's cumulative performance portfolio.

In appendix A, we have included completed monitoring reports developed by a number of clients. Our author's notes at the top of each example provide further guidance as you review the reports. One caution: While we believe all examples represent thoughtful work, none is perfect. Readers are encouraged to use the examples as starting points for their own work.

ADVICE FOR THE CEO ABOUT OE MONITORING

Building a quality monitoring report requires the CEO and supporting staff members to take the responsibility seriously. It is an important exercise, not only because it serves as the basis for the board's judgment of the organization's performance, but also because it provides the opportunity for the staff to examine the real condition of every operational function at least once each year.

When reports are developed, we suggest that the CEO:

- *Use a consistent format,* following the content steps we outlined at the top of this section and reflected in the examples (see exhibit 4.1). Present the steps in their *natural order* as shown, and draw from the samples later in this chapter (some of which are abbreviated due to length). Board members must be able to understand quickly and easily what the reports contain without having to sift through multiple presentation formats and styles.
- *Treat each sub-part of the policy as a separate policy.* Each deserves its own interpretation, indicators, and evidence of compliance.
- *Be absolutely, brutally honest in stating compliance.* If the organization is not in compliance, say so. The board must be able to rely on the CEO's word. It takes only one instance of falsifying a report to destroy the board's confidence in both the process and the CEO. *It usually is not a capital offense to be out of compliance; it is to intentionally mislead or falsify information!*
- *Adhere to timelines.* If the board's annual work plan calls for a report to be provided by a given date, don't let that date pass without submitting it.
- *Avoid presenting process disguised as evidence.* This is the number one problem we see with OE monitoring reports. The CEO and staff are eager to let the board know all the wonderful things the organization is doing. None of that matters here. What the board expects is solid evidence that all

those great things the staff is doing actually worked. The monitoring report should let the board know that they did. That means that compliance must be demonstrated by actual performance data, not process and a list of staff activities.

- *If reports do include process information*, it should be clearly labeled as such: *incidental information* or *for board information only*. If this option to reveal process is chosen, the CEO should include information that the CEO believes will further educate the board.

  The OE monitoring report can be a very effective vehicle to share information about processes and practices that otherwise the board would never know. The wise CEO will take advantage of this opportunity, but without burying the board in paper.

  But it should be recognized that *process does not equal evidence*. Do not confuse activity with compliance results.
- *Capacity building (optional)*. Listing capacities that the organization needs to improve can be useful, especially if the organization is noncompliant in a given area due to limited capacity. It can be helpful to share with the board the conditions that must change in order for compliance to be achieved. Such information should identify the needed resources, and the projected timeframe, necessary for the organization to achieve and document full compliance or to further improve operational performance and accountability.

DISPOSE OF REPORTS ON THE CONSENT AGENDA OR AS SEPARATE ACTION ITEMS?

Some boards prefer to discuss each OE monitoring report before taking action. Others choose to approve reports as part of the consent agenda if members are completely satisfied with the report and the CEO's performance.

Which is correct? *They both are.*

Consent Agenda

We have counseled boards that if there is nothing to talk about, don't talk about it. This saves valuable time for the board to use on more important issues that do require discussion. If the board is satisfied with both the condition of the organization's operations and with the quality of the monitoring report, there is nothing wrong with disposing of the reports as part of the consent agenda.

However, even if the board does act on OE reports via the consent agenda, the CEO is entitled to some response from the board to close the communication loop. The president or chairman should document board acceptance based on the board's consent action.

Discussion Agenda

For boards that do feel the need to discuss each report before passing judgment, there is nothing wrong with that option either. Boards should discuss each report during the first couple of monitoring cycles at least, to be sure of both policy content and monitoring sufficiency.

This is the learning period. It is important for both the board and CEO to take the time to review and discuss each report openly to gain familiarity with the policy content and to establish an acceptable level of communication between the parties.

Getting to Results

We caution boards against dwelling too long and too intently on this "new toy." Some boards can consume themselves with OE monitoring, and as a result find themselves back in a place they said they wanted to leave: mired in the intimate details of organizational operations.

As a rule of thumb, OE monitoring should not take more board meeting time than the board's attention to Results. If OE monitoring seems to be the centerpiece of the board's meeting, the board probably is too focused on OE monitoring—unless operationally something seriously is not working.

CEO or Organization Evaluation?

What the board is doing when it acts on an OE monitoring report is expressing its satisfaction—or lack thereof—with the *organization's* performance. Since the board's policy states that the organization's performance and the CEO's performance are identical, both are being evaluated simultaneously.

However, the starting point for OE monitoring is a review of the organization's performance. This initial focus on organizational performance prevents the evaluation—sometimes publicly—of the CEO every time the board meets. The CEO's personal evaluation will occur in closed session when the summative evaluation is conducted.

This issue is discussed more fully in chapter 6.

PRESENTING THE MONITORING REPORT

There is something of an art to effectively presenting and acting on a monitoring report, for both Operational Expectations and Results policies. Most boards have not previously engaged in a process quite like this, so it can feel awkward at first.

This awkward phase should pass very quickly, however, once the board gains comfort as a result of doing it a time or two. The best way we have found to effectively dispose of monitoring reports is to follow established parliamentary procedure, according to the processes recommended below.

The process example that follows assumes that the report being presented is a formal monitoring report, including acceptance of both interpretation and compliance data, as outlined at the beginning of this chapter.

The president begins the board's consideration by contextualizing the report, introducing it with comments similar to the following:

> The board has established through its Operational Expectations policies its values about how this organization is expected to operate. We have clearly expressed the conditions that must exist as business takes place.
>
> We now are going to receive a monitoring report on one Operational Expectations policy (OE-2, Planning for Executive Succession). We will receive the report containing the CEO's interpretation of our language, a certification of compliance, and monitoring data. This monitoring action constitutes our rigorous oversight of the organization and assures the board that its operational policies are being complied with. I now recognize (CEO) for the purpose of presenting a summary of the report.

The CEO "tees up" the report by stating the operational area being monitored, and reminds the board of the action being requested of it. The CEO presents a brief summary of the report, or s/he may introduce a staff member who had "point position" for preparing it. The CEO should not read the report to the board, but rather summarize it by highlighting its important points and conclusions—an executive summary. Board members should not interrupt the CEO's presentation, but save their questions and comments until the overview is complete.

AFTER THE REPORT HAS BEEN PRESENTED

Following the overview of the report, before any Q and A from the board, the president should remind the board of its policy standard for accepting these reports (BCR-5) with a statement similar to the following:

> Members of the board have received the CEO's monitoring report on OE-__. Now it is the board's responsibility to consider the report as evidence of organization performance in this area of operations. Following a motion and second to accept, I will invite any member of the board who has questions or comments about the report to offer them to the CEO.
>
> Let me remind the board of the criteria we should use to judge this report. They are whether the board is satisfied that:
>
> 1. The CEO's interpretation of the policy is reasonable;
> 2. The CEO has provided sufficient evidence to assure the board that the organization is in compliance with the provisions of the policy;
> 3. Or, if noncompliance is being reported, whether the CEO has disclosed procedures and a timeline to establish compliance.
>
> I encourage members to limit their questions and comments to these criteria. Do I have a motion to accept the report as presented?

Following that motion and second, the board then is free to discuss the report.

In order to start board discussion of a monitoring report, we recommend a motion similar to the following:

> President ___, I move to accept the CEO's monitoring report on OE-__ as presented.

This motion will serve the board well, even if there are interpretation or compliance issues to be considered. The routine amendment process may be used to express any such concerns.

If your board is a public board, such as a school board, we recommend having a written executive summary of the report available for audience members to use to follow your discussion. You might also consider projecting the relevant policy on large, readable screens.

Follow parliamentary procedure. Faithfully start the discussion with a motion and second, as suggested above, in order to frame the discussion and possible amending motions leading to final board action.

After board discussion and action, the final vote is recorded on the cover of the OE report. That action should be one of three possible options:

1. *In compliance*
2. *Not in compliance*, with a defined follow-up date for re-monitoring
3. *In compliance, with noted exceptions.* This means that any policy sub-parts reported as noncompliant, or any sub-parts excluded by the board from the motion to accept, are scheduled for re-monitoring at a defined time.

If a re-monitoring date is determined, it is added to the board's annual work plan immediately. This assures the board that the necessary follow-up action will take place. The administrative assistant to the board, or the board clerk, will find that the annual work plan could change at every meeting of the board.

SOME POINTS TO CONSIDER

- *Remember, again, that the standard of organization performance the board has set in policy is reasonable, not perfection.* Both the board and staff are doing something they never have done before, and some less-than-perfect work is to be expected in the early going.

In some cases, the organization may be performing in a very compliant manner, but lack the organizational capacity at this early stage to prove it. Thus the message to both the board and staff is to be tolerant of each other as this process is being institutionalized.

This is not to suggest that clearly substandard performance be accepted. This is a serious process, and it deserves the CEO's best effort to produce a quality monitoring report, fairly documenting the true condition of the organization's operational performance.

Assuming the CEO has given a good-faith effort, the board might recognize that effort, and state its expectation that the reports will get better and documentation will become stronger when presented the second and third times.

- *We remind the CEO that no report should be read to the board.* Assume that each member has done the required homework. Provide an executive summary of the important points contained in the report.
- To both board and CEO, remember that *this monitoring process is not intended to be a negative event, or an opportunity to catch someone doing something wrong.* It is intended to be an opportunity to critically but constructively examine what is working as expected and where new attention might be needed.
- If the report acknowledges noncompliance with any part of the policy, the *CEO also should inform the board of specific plans to remedy the noncompliant condition and the timeline necessary to achieve compliance.* Board acceptance of the report includes its acknowledgment of the noncompliant conditions and its agreement with the timeline for remedy.
- *Avoid using the reports as opportunities to second-guess the CEO or to do the CEO's work for him or her.* We again caution the board against spending

an inordinate amount of time disposing of OE reports. Take as much time as reasonably necessary to be sure you understand what the report says and whether you are convinced that organizational performance is reasonably compliant.

- *Remember one critical point: The board's job is not to substitute its opinions for those of the CEO.* The task is to either accept the report as presented, accept the parts considered compliant and exclude (by amendment) the parts considered to be noncompliant, or return the entire report to the CEO for additional work. If the board substitutes its own opinions and ideas for those of the CEO, it is doing the CEO's work. That is something that never should happen.
- *If the board considers parts of the report to be noncompliant, they are excluded by amendment from the compliance motion and a date for re-monitoring those parts of the policy should be established.* Dialog between the board and CEO assures a reasonable timeline for re-monitoring the report. It is placed on the board's annual work plan to assure that it does not fall between the cracks.

SAMPLE MOTIONS FOR DISPOSING OF OE REASONABLE INTERPRETATION REPORTS

1. *Initial motion* (to accept the report and begin consideration):
   "Mr./Madam President, I move that the board accept the CEO's reasonable interpretation and indicators for OE-__ as presented."
   - ✓ Second, then discuss and vote
2. *Possible amending motion* (if part(s) of the report are considered to be unreasonable):
   "Mr./Madam President, I move to amend the motion by excluding (insert specific part of report the mover believes to be unreasonable)."
   - ✓ Second, then discuss and vote
   - ✓ Specific details should be offered by the mover to justify the change
   - ✓ A date for possible re-monitoring of the exception is scheduled
3. *Possible amending motion* (if additional information is needed):
   "Mr./Madam President, I move to amend the motion by excluding Section _____ of the report from the main motion, and informing the CEO that additional (or different) information will be necessary for the board to determine reasonableness, and further that the requested information be provided to the board by _____."

✓ Second, then discuss and vote

✓ Specific details about additional information being requested should be identified

SAMPLE MOTIONS FOR APPROVAL OF OE MONITORING REPORT

1. *Initial motion* (to accept the report and begin consideration):
   "Mr./Madam President, I move that the board accept the CEO's monitoring report on OE-__, as presented, as evidence of the status of compliance with the provisions of the policy."

   ✓ Second, then discuss and vote
2. *Possible amending motion* (if part(s) of the report are considered to be unreasonable or noncompliant, despite the CEO's certification of compliance):
   "Mr./Madam President, I move to amend the motion by excluding (insert specific part of report the mover believes to be unreasonable or noncompliant) from the motion to accept."

   ✓ Second, then discuss and vote

   a. Specific details should be offered by the mover to justify the change

   b. A date for possible re-monitoring of the exception is scheduled
3. *Possible amending motion* (if additional information is needed):
   "Mr./Madam President, I move to amend the motion by excluding Section __ of the report from the main motion, and informing the CEO that additional (or different) information will be necessary for the board to determine compliance, and further that the requested information be provided to the board by __."

   ✓ Second, then discuss and vote

   a. Specific details about additional information being requested should be identified

   b. The date for any re-monitoring should be placed on the board's annual work plan for follow-up

Clear documentation of how the board disposed of the report and why it reached that conclusion become indispensable when the time comes to review all reports during the CEO evaluation. The sample monitoring reports contained in the appendices are intended to help your board start its journey toward a meaningful experience in this important segment of implementation.

ORGANIZING STAFF

Well before the first report is written by the CEO and presented to the board, the CEO must organize the staff to support the process. How to do that is dependent largely on the size of the staff and the complexity of the organization. The staff alignment chart in exhibit 4.2 was developed by one CEO to guide the staff's work as they prepared reports for ultimate presentation to the board.

EXHIBIT 4.2

Sample OE Monitoring Reports Preparation Schedule, Sorted Chronologically

OE Policy	**Staff Respon-sible (assigned by CEO)**	**Date for Review by Cabinet**	**Date Due to Board (approxi-mately 2 weeks prior to meeting)**	**Date to be on Board Agenda**
OE-2: Emergency Superin-tendent Succession	Able	Monday July 21	Friday July 25	August 11
OE-5: Staff Compensa-tion	Blake	Monday August 18	Friday August 22	September 8
OE-7: Budgeting/ Financial Planning	Clark	September 1	Friday September 5	September 22
OPEN FOR MONI-TORING EXCEP-TIONS	XXXXX	Monday September 22	Friday September 26	October 13

OE Policy	Staff Responsible (assigned by CEO)	Date for Review by Cabinet	Date Due to Board (approximately 2 weeks prior to meeting)	Date to be on Board Agenda
OE-10: Communication and Counsel to the Board	Dolan	Monday October 6	Friday October 10	October 27
OE-6: Staff Evaluation	Echols	Monday October 20	Friday October 24	November 10
Monitor Non-TAKS Measures	Frank	Monday November 3	Friday November 7	November 10
OE-12: Curriculum and Instruction	Grant	Monday November 3	Friday November 7	November 24
OE-11: Annual Report to the Public	Harris	Monday November 17	Friday November 21	December 8
OE-1: Global Executive Constraint	Irby	Monday December 8	Friday December 12 (Prior to Winter Break)	January 12
OE-9: Asset Protection	Jackson	Tuesday January 6	Friday January 9	January 26
OE-14: District Calendar	Kelly	Tuesday January 20	Friday January 23	February 9

In some organizations of modest size, this degree of staff delegation may not be possible. But in larger organizations, it is desirable to create as many opportunities as possible for first- and second-tier staff members to engage in the process. This involvement builds capacity and ownership by involving good minds in support of the entire organizational response to the board's work.

Planning this process should begin with the end in mind. By what date should the report be delivered to the board in sufficient time for members to read, study, and analyze the content? How much time should be planned for board members to ask any questions for clarification prior to the meeting at which the report will be presented and deliberated? Board members commonly expect a week to ten days to study monitoring reports.

As staff work schedules are developed, the CEO should consider designating a point person to be responsible for each report, based on logical staff responsibilities and organizational alignment. The draft report should be submitted to the administrative cabinet or senior leadership team for critique and group feedback in time to permit revisions before it is submitted to the board. After cabinet review, some boards send the resulting report to consultants for "third-eye" feedback before it is finalized and submitted to the board.

This is a time when the board's administrative assistant or other designated support person is invaluable in making sure that all staff reports are prepared on time to deliver according to the board's annual work plan. Someone must be designated to quarterback this entire process, to drive it according to schedule. If that person isn't the CEO, he or she must have sufficient authority to require other staff members to deliver the necessary documents at the required time. Otherwise, the best of schedules on paper becomes a meaningless exercise.

Appendix A is a compilation of several reports and partial reports, all worthy of study. Keep in mind that these are *samples,* and not always perfect examples of how reports should be developed. We do point out on some of them what technically is good and what we would recommend be done differently. This is an opportunity to learn from the work of others and reduce time, effort, and potential errors in developing your own reports as you move into good governance practices.

Questions for Thought

1. Do you believe the board will know more, or less, about the operations of the organization as a result of these OE monitoring reports?
2. What was the standard for operational performance under your old governance system?
3. Under your old governance system, how did you know when things failed to work as expected?

FAQs

Q: Isn't requiring the CEO and staff to struggle with an interpretation a waste of staff time when the words in the policy seem quite clear on their face?

A: No. Words mean something—and sometimes something different—from one person to another. The interpretation is important because it assures the board that communication of the same value has occurred and that organizational response to the board's policy will be acceptable to the board. The time to determine whether interpretations are reasonable is before any missteps occur, not afterward.

Q: What is wrong with the CEO's telling the board about operational activities and strategies when these reports are presented?

A: There is nothing wrong with including process information in the reports, provided that information is not confused with evidence of compliance. Process does not equate with compliance data. If process information is included in reports, it should be clearly labeled as such, and it should not be the dominant part of the report.

Q: Do OE reports add any real value to the staff or the organization?

A: As one CEO of a billion-dollar organization told us, OE reports require him to deliberately and proactively examine every aspect of the organization at least annually. The process of opening up everything to verify that all decisions are made in compliance with a stated value system allows him to have systemic and systematic knowledge, making corrections to problems that otherwise would not have been diagnosed until there was trouble. OE policies are operating standards for every facet of organizational activity. If they are viewed as such, they can be of enormous value to the organization and the people whose jobs are to make things work well.

Chapter 5

Monitoring Results Policies

The reason for any organization to exist is to provide benefits for the people it serves. Sometimes board behavior can suggest that the primary reason for the board's existence is to obsess about the most elaborate buildings, or the employee compensation package, or the most detailed finance system, or something else that has all to do with operations. These concerns are not why the organization exists.

The issues on which boards spend most of their time—the matters that dominate their meetings, and the topics they dwell on the most—reflect the things they believe to be most important. Far too often, those things are operational in nature, as opposed to outcome focused.

To be fair, however, those operational matters are much more familiar to board members than outcome issues are. They are much more easily discussed than whether customers and owners are getting from the organization those benefits they expect and need. Board members tend to understand (or think they do) facilities, personnel, budgets, and balance sheets based on their own professions or interests. For school boards, discussing whether all students are achieving at the levels they should is a different challenge.

Nevertheless, outcome obsession should be the hallmark of a good board. This isn't meant to suggest that efficient and effective operations are unimportant. But it is to recognize that all those operational matters mean little if the organization fails to produce the outcomes it exists to provide. And it is the job of the board to assure that it does.

The board, whose members serve as trustees for the owners who themselves are not at the table or dais, often must weigh conflicting values about results. They will find themselves making tough choices about which elements of the organization's client base should receive which benefit. The board must struggle with the decision of whether benefiting specific subgroups ultimately benefits the whole—despite the fact that other subgroups the board serves may disagree with board choices to "favor" any particular subgroups. The challenge is to serve, to lead, and to represent all subgroups for the ultimate health and common good of the whole.

The board determines in policy the Results to be achieved. Once the board has determined *what* must be achieved, it then delegates to the CEO and staff all decisions related to *how* the results are to be achieved. But CEO and staff choices must be made within the decision-making latitude defined by the board in its Operational Expectations policies.

Priorities within and among Results may be established to forge organiztional focus. These priorities may and will shift and change as circumstances evolve, based on the actual performance of the organization.

All of this works if the board is diligent in performing its critical role in this exchange: effectively monitoring Results progress. Quality Results monitoring allows the board to:

- Monitor the progress being made incrementally by the organization to achieve the board's Results;
- Build a portfolio of CEO performance in the Results half of the CEO's job expectations.

MONITORING PROCESS

Not unexpectedly, the process for monitoring Results may involve a variety of options. But regardless of the choice of processes, all quality Results monitoring reports should contain a consistent set of elements that includes:

- Restatement of the board's policy (or the particular sub-part being monitored);
- The CEO's literal interpretation of that policy language;
- The specific indicators to be used to measure progress;
- Baseline performance data for each indicator, the starting point against which progress will be measured;
- Short-term and long-term performance targets for each indicator; and finally, at a future point on the calendar; and
- Monitoring data to indicate whether actual performance matched targets established for each chosen indicator.

None of these steps can be eliminated. As was the case with Operational Expectations monitoring, we recommend a two-step process for the first cycle of Results policy monitoring. The first step should consist of the reasonable interpretation, indicators, baseline (or current level of performance for each indicator), and proposed targets.

The task is to measure reasonable progress, and thus the board must know that the interpretation of its policy language is reasonable and that the indicators and both short-term and long-term performance targets selected by the CEO are reasonable. This sets the stage for strategic decision-making by the CEO and staff, with assurance that the board and CEO share common understanding about the reasonableness of these critical components.

Baseline data is what it is; there is no reason for the board to approve that. However, the CEO's choice of performance targets is a matter that should be approved by the board in advance of actual monitoring in order to assure that both the CEO and the board agree on the definition of "reasonable" progress.

Once the board and CEO have reached a point of shared understanding of all these components, and in the process reached common agreement about what "reasonable" looks like, the stage is set for effective and efficient (and one would hope noncontroversial) monitoring of actual organizational performance.

Formal monitoring usually occurs a year or so after the preparation steps have been taken. This final step must be separated from the initial preliminary steps by at least some reasonable time span in order to allow staff to gear up for the measurement of progress. They will use the interpretations, indicators, and performance targets previously accepted by the board as the basis for their assessment of that progress. During the first year of implementation for most organizations, this second step in Results monitoring usually comes a year or so following the first step.

After the first complete cycle of Results monitoring, these two steps can be merged into a single step. The interpretations are unlikely to change significantly from one period to another. However, it is not unusual for indicators to change if some prove not to work as well as expected, or if others need to be added over time. The baseline will not change for existing indicators, but performance targets could be adjusted at each monitoring cycle, depending on actual results.

If performance data indicate that reasonable progress has not been made either overall or by subgroup exceptions, the CEO in the monitoring report is expected to reveal to the board the factors that led to such failure and the actions that are contemplated as means to improve organizational performance.

If new resources are needed, if new strategies are necessary, or if different actions are required that currently exceed organizational capacity, this is the place to so inform the board. Such information frequently is presented to the board in a final category of the monitoring report called "Capacity Building." It is not expected to be used as a catch-all for offering excuses for organizational failure, but rather as a place to inform the board of resources that may be necessary for continued progress.

JUDGING REASONABLE PROGRESS

Here is the tricky part for all boards: If all pre-approved targets were hit, little judgment about reasonable organizational progress should be necessary; by definition, the organization's progress would be considered reasonable. But what if some, but not all, targets were hit? What if the trend line moved in the right direction, but targets were not hit? What if the overall monitoring numbers looked relatively bleak, but some external factors over which the organization had little or no control played a significant part in those results?

Regardless of what the numbers are, the board still has work to do, and will be challenged to *reasonably* use the data that are presented and weigh the results against all known factors to reach a fair and reasonable assessment of organizational progress. We can make every effort to quantify success and try to take all the possible guesswork out of the process. But in the end, reasonable people must make the best decision they can, using the best information they have, to fairly judge organizational performance.

Regardless of the process leading to the final monitoring report, once the report is presented, the board must formally act by deciding from among the following choices:

- Reasonable progress has been achieved;
- Reasonable progress has not been achieved, or insufficient data have been provided to make a judgment;
- Reasonable progress has been made, with specified exception(s).

The board's action should be recorded on the cover of the monitoring report (samples are included in appendix B), along with the CEO certification of accuracy and status of progress. We recommend that any board action to offer commendations for extraordinary performance or direction for improvement be added in a comment section. This serves as a record of the board's disposition of the report and informs board discussion during the CEO's summative evaluation.

Board disposition of the monitoring report closes the loop on that particular monitoring event. The monitoring document and report become a part of the CEO's cumulative performance portfolio, and will be a part of the summative evaluation later in the year.

A word of caution to boards as they assess organizational performance. *Improvement will not always move in a straight, upward trajectory.* It is reasonable to set targets and try diligently to meet them for every indicator every year. But our real-world experiences tell us that that will not happen.

At any given measurement point, it is logical to expect to see more progress in some areas or with some groups than others. And it is predictable that some indicators will show increases while others may not. What the board should look for is performance over time. Are the trend lines moving in the right direction? Are there justifiable reasons why they are not? What steps are being taken to improve? What are the targets for next year, and should they be adjusted based on this year's performance?

These are the questions a board should ask. And if the Result policy calls for 100 percent performance, it may never be achieved. This means that the board always must be reasonable in its determination of reasonable progress.

As was the case with OE monitoring, what the board is doing when it acts on a Results monitoring report is expressing its satisfaction—or lack thereof—with the *organization's* performance.

Since the board's policy states that the organization's performance and the CEO's performance are identical, then, of course, both are being evaluated simultaneously. However, the starting point for the board's Results monitoring is a review of the organization's performance, knowing that at some point in the future the CEO will be credited with the results of that action. This initial focus on organizational performance prevents the evaluation of the CEO at every meeting. The CEO's personal evaluation will occur in closed session when the summative evaluation is conducted. Chapter 6 discusses this CEO evaluation topic in greater depth.

RESULTS MONITORING GUIDELINES FOR THE CEO

Because of the high level of importance assigned to Results monitoring and the significant impact the process can have throughout the organization (as well as on the CEO's own evaluation), the CEO should take this challenge as one of the most important jobs of the CEO and key staff. We offer these words of guidance to the CEO about how to build these reports.

1. *Certify the accuracy* of the report. Certify to the board that the information contained in the report is true and accurate. It usually is not fatal to fail to make reasonable progress. It is fatal to provide a report that lacks full integrity and accuracy.
2. *Provide an executive summary, including:*
   a. *An analysis of the data:* What did the data tell staff about performance across the organization? What did it fail to reveal?
   b. *Clear indication of whether targets were met:* Was reasonable progress still achieved, even it targets were not met?
   c. *Capacity building:* Are further data points required to effectively measure progress? Does the organization need additional resources to achieve the Result? Is the cost reasonable for the return? Over what period of time?
3. *Provide a glossary of terms* to include any terminology unique to your industry, keeping in mind that board members may not be proficient in the terminology of the organization.
4. *Restate the policy and its sub-parts* as the preface to your interpretation. Don't make the board cross-reference the policy to the report. Keep the flow of the report sequential, logical, and simple.
5. *Provide a literal interpretation of the policy and sub-policy statements.* Is the CEO's interpretation of the board's policy language reasonable and consistent with the board's value? Have you captured the core concern as the board stated it? Have you over-interpreted—adding your own values—or wandered into process? And remember, simply restating the words used in the policy fails as an interpretation.
6. *Identify indicators of performance.* By indicators, we mean observable behaviors, actions, or documentable results that will constitute performance measures. Sometimes assessment tools, metrics, or tests can constitute indicators. For example, an indicator of progress for a school organization may be tests that measure academic performance. Indicators for other, "non-academic" Results will be less precise and more difficult to determine, but they are equally important.
7. *Baseline current performance for each indicator.* In order to measure progress, the organization must know where it is now. The CEO must baseline current performance for each indicator to allow concrete determination about whether reasonable gain has been achieved at some point in the future. If an insurance pool board values a confidence level of 90 percent and the current level is 80 percent, progress should be measured against the 80 percent, the baseline.
8. *Set incremental targets, or goals, for each indicator.* If students are graduating at a 60 percent level at the point of baseline, and the ultimate

Result policy expects 100 percent, incremental targets stretching toward 100 percent should be set and measured against longitudinally, over time. We recommend both short-term, such as one year, and longer-term targets, such as five years out.

9. *Monitor reasonable progress.* Have the targets been achieved using the indicators you selected? If so, celebrate and establish new targets. If not, why not? And then, under a heading called Process, indicate what you intend to do about it.

In instances of failure to achieve reasonable progress, the CEO should identify where the problem areas are, what changes the organization anticipates making, and the time and resources needed to meet the targets.

QUESTIONS TO ANTICIPATE AND ENCOURAGE THE BOARD TO EXPLORE

1. *Indicators:* Is one indicator of performance sufficient? Is one high-stakes assessment sufficient to judge performance? If not, are others available? Which indicators are useful as formative assessments and which are realistically summative?
2. *Targets:* How were they established? Why are you projecting the same or different percentage improvements for different subgroups? How valid is benchmarking against other organizations or geographic areas?
3. Why did any one subgroup improve so dramatically?

SHARING STRATEGIES TO ACHIEVE INCREASED PERFORMANCE

Other than the sharing of all letters except for a "c" and "gr," the words "process" and "progress" have nothing in common. Yet, when we review Results (and even Operational Expectations) monitoring reports, it is clear that some CEOs and staff members seem to consider the two words to be almost interchangeable. Processes used by organizations far too frequently are disguised as either compliance in the case of Operational Expectations reports, or as progress in the case of Results reports.

This is one of the most frequent criticisms we have of staff efforts to effectively produce reports to the board documenting reasonable progress with Results policies. If the CEO and staff religiously follow the monitoring sequence we discussed earlier in this chapter, there should be no confusion about what is process and what is evidence of progress.

Yet invariably CEOs and staff members want desperately to inform the board of all the good work they are doing, and all the great strategies and activities the organization has in place. And of course, most boards are eager to learn about all these neat things that are happening in the operational side of the organization.

In the final analysis, there is nothing wrong with the board's knowing these things. In fact, board knowledge of organizational programs and strategies can help the board perform its advocacy role in support of the organization and where it is headed.

But the question is whether the Results monitoring report is the place to share such operational information. As we discussed earlier, if monitoring data reveal that reasonable progress has not been made, the board likely expects to know what will change in order to produce better results. So at least in this case, strategic and programmatic information will find its way into the report.

But it must be separated very obviously from monitoring data, and it must be called what it is: process information. The board never should be confused about the information it is using to make judgments about organizational performance. Mixing operational activities with Results performance data can have that outcome, and must be avoided. If and when operational activity information is presented as a part of a Results monitoring report, it should be presented under a separate heading, clearly labeled as, for example, "*Program and Strategic Information: Incidental Only.*"

The message here: Take every precaution against inviting the board back into the world of organizational strategy. That is the world of the CEO and staff. The board has good reason to want to know about the important operational decisions that are being made. But the board now lives in the world of governance, not operations. The CEO must take care not to lead the board into the staff's domain, or confuse the role clarity that Coherent Governance® achieves.

SOME ADDITIONAL SUGGESTIONS FOR THE CEO

When presenting Results monitoring reports to the board, the CEO should:

1. Provide organization-wide aggregated performance data based on all monitoring indicators previously accepted by the board. Supplement this information with disaggregated data, depending on the specific subgroups served by your organization.

2. To the extent possible, include data illustrating progress over time. Longitudinal charts are helpful and meet the increasing desire of most boards to see performance trends year-to-year.
3. List conclusions to be drawn from the data. Note strengths as well as weaknesses. When significant, describe and explain performance differences among subgroups, as well as the organization's failure to hit performance targets.
4. Note any concerns about the validity or reliability of the data.

   Note to the board: The board should be skilled at understanding data and its application to the specifics of the clients the organization serves. If it is not, new skills must be developed to improve board capacity to do its job. This is a point where new governance methods can fall apart. Boards often tend not to invest in their own development, skills and knowledge to perform their job with excellence.

5. Point out performance data that reveal problem areas. Describe program deficiencies that need to be addressed and how you intend to improve. These are means and should not become the focus of the report. See the precautions about merging means information (strategies and actions) with results monitoring reports discussed earlier.
6. Distribute the completed report to the board at least one week in advance of the presentation.
7. Do not read the report to the board. Members are expected to come to meetings fully prepared. Verbally summarize the report, and call attention to any significant points.
8. If there is a large amount of information to be considered, spread the presentation across two or more board meetings.
9. Be sure the text is concise, understandable, and supplemented by clear graphics.
10. Present the data, along with your analysis. In other words, interpret what the data have told you and your staff. What did it fail to tell you? What other data sources (indicators) may be necessary? What capacity building may be necessary?

The CEO logically will delegate the development of monitoring reports to the staff member(s) with the greatest level of responsibility in specific Results areas. Nevertheless, vetting these reports through the senior staff or administrative cabinet provides opportunities to refine the reports before they go to the board.

Exhibit 5.1 is a sample staff report development timeline created by one school superintendent and his chief of staff.

EXHIBIT 5.1

Staff Schedule for Preparation of Monitoring Reports

RESULT	Point Person	Draft to Cabinet	Final to Cabinet	Report to CEO Secretary	Report Sent to the Board	Board Meeting
R-1 Mission (M) R-2 Literacy (I)	Adams					Mon June 30
R-2 Numeracy (I)	Black	Mon July 14	Fri July 18	Mon July 21	Mon July 28	Mon July 28
R-2 Technology(I)	Clark	Thurs July 31	Fri Aug 8	Mon Aug 11	Fri Aug 22	Wed August 27
R-2 Academic Performance (M) R-4 Character (I) R-3 Citizenship(I)	Dale	Mon Sept 8	Fri Sept 12	Mon Sept 15	Fri Sept 26	Mon Sept 29
R-2 Science (I) R-6 Balanced and Healthy Lives (I)	Ellis	Tues Oct 7	Tues Oct 14	Tues Oct 14	Thurs Oct 23	Mon Oct 27
R-2 Social Studies (I)	Frank	Fri Oct 31	Tues Nov 11	Mon Nov 10	Fri Nov 21	Mon Nov 24
R-2 Visual and Performing Arts (I)	Grant	Fri Dec 5	Fri Dec 12	Mon Dec 8	Fri Dec 19	Mon Dec 22

R-3 Citizenship (M) R-2 World Languages (I)	Hall	Fri Dec 19	Fri Jan 9	Mon Jan 12	Fri Jan 23	Mon January 26
R-6 Balanced and Healthy Lives (M) R-2 Health/ PE (I)	Imry	Tues Jan 27	Mon Feb 9	Thurs Feb 12	Fri Feb 20	Mon Feb 23
R-4 Character (M)	Johns	Mon Mar 1	Fri Mar 12	Mon Mar 15	Fri Mar 26	Mon March 29
No Report						April
R-5 Workplace Performance (M)	Kelly	Fri April 30	Fri May 7	Mon May 10	Fri May 21	Mon May 24
RI = Reasonable Interpretation I = Indicators B = Baseline T = Targets M = Monitoring Reasonable Progress						

RECEIVING AND DISPOSING OF REPORTS

The art of receiving and responding to reports is not magical, but it is important. Remember, by the time a report gets to the board, the CEO and staff have invested considerable time and effort in building a document they believe fairly represents the organization's performance. The reports and staff members who prepared them deserve due consideration within the framework of what the board is there to decide.

Both the CEO and the board president should establish clear context for receiving a report and what is expected from the board. What is the board being asked to do? Is the board being asked to accept the interpretation and indicators as reasonable? Accept the proposed targets? Accept the evidence of reasonable progress?

Following are two sample statements that clarify for the board, staff, and audience exactly what the report is intended to accomplish.

Sample 1: President's Statement to Open Discussion to Consider Results Interpretation, Indicators, and Targets

"Members of the board have received and reviewed the CEO's Reasonable Interpretation report on R-___. It now is the board's responsibility to consider the reasonableness of this interpretation, including the choice of indicators and targets, to demonstrate performance in this Results area.

After a motion and second to accept the report, I will invite any member of the board who has questions or comments about the report to offer them to the CEO or his designee. Let me remind the board that the standards for acting on the report are:

1. whether the board is satisfied that the policy and its subparts have been reasonably interpreted;
2. whether the board is satisfied that the organization and the CEO have selected reasonable indicators to demonstrate progress and have set reasonable performance targets based on current baseline data.

I encourage members to limit their questions and comments to these criteria."

Sample 2: President's Statement to Open Board Discussion of Results Progress Monitoring Report

"Members of the board have received and reviewed the CEO's monitoring report on R-___. It now is the board's responsibility to consider the report as evidence of reasonable organizational progress in this Results area.

"Following a motion and second to accept the report, I will invite any member of the board who has questions or comments about the report to offer them to the CEO or his designee. Let me remind the board that our task is to decide whether the report provides sufficient evidence that the organization has made reasonable progress toward achieving this Result. I encourage members to limit their questions and comments to this topic."

Receiving the Report

After the president has "teed up" the report, the CEO then is expected to either present an overview of the report or introduce a key member of the staff to do so. The task of the point person who assumes that responsibility is not to read the report, but to offer a summary of the highlights and the conclusions. This verbal executive summary should anticipate the board's questions and concerns, depending on the results that have been achieved, and provide answers to questions as well as they can be anticipated. Any further clarity about what is expected of the board should be discussed as well.

After this staff summary of the report, the next action that should be taken is the president's call for a motion to accept the report, before any board discussion of it. Beginning the discussion with a formal motion helps focus the conversation on the question. It minimizes the board's temptation to wander around in various aspects of the report or become distracted by other, extraneous issues that have little to do with the board's task: to judge reasonable progress.

We recommend starting the process with a "clean" motion to accept the report as presented, even if members of the board have issues with certain parts of it. Those concerns may be expressed via the amendment process after deliberation begins. To try to start the board's discussion with a motion that includes both acceptance of the report and exceptions to it confuses the board's conversation—and it is a violation of accepted parliamentary procedure.

Of course, if the board is convinced that the report simply isn't ready for prime time, an opening motion could be made to postpone consideration until a later date or some such motion. Normally, however, if the board is prepared to receive and act on the report, the simple *motion to accept* will start that discussion very effectively.

Following is a sample motion to be used to accept the report and to begin the process of deliberation, using standard parliamentary procedure.

Sample Motion to Initiate Consideration of Results Monitoring Reports

1. *Initial motion*
   "Mr./Madam President, I move that the board accept the CEO's report on R__, as presented."
   ✓ Second, then discuss and vote
2. *Possible amending motion* (offered by an individual member who disagrees with the reasonableness of the CEO's interpretation, indicators, targets, or assertion of progress):
   "Mr./Madam President, I move to amend the motion by ____________."
   ✓ Second, then discuss and vote

SAMPLE FORMS

Below are two sample report covers that may be used to memorialize and summarize the board's actions on reports. Sample one:

Author's Note: This is a simple, clear document for the board to complete after action on a monitoring report. It establishes a record of the board's disposition and future expectations.

RESULTS MONITORING REPORT RESPONSE FORM

Policy Number and Title: ____

____________________________, Chair ____________________________, CEO

Disposition of the Board: Date: ______ Date for Re-monitoring: ______

The board on the date indicated above reviewed the monitoring report of this policy and reached the following conclusion:

1. _______ *Reasonable progress is being made.* The board commends the organization and the CEO for exemplary performance in the following areas:

   ____

   ____

2. _______ *Reasonable progress has been achieved, with the following exceptions.*

   ____

Accordingly, the board requires the following:

____

3. ______ *Reasonable progress has not been demonstrated or insufficient data have been presented* to make a determination as to whether reasonable progress has been made. Accordingly, the board requires the following for re-monitoring:

____

____

____

The second sample memorializes the board's action in the two-step reporting process. The form below allows the board to record its approval of the interpretation, indicators, and targets as its first action, as well as the approval of reasonable progress at a later time.

Organization Name/Date
Comprehensive Results Monitoring Report

Results			
Results (#):		Title	

I certify this report to be accurate. ______________________, CEO

Results Vote		
Check One	**Nature of Monitoring Report**	**Scheduled Date for Board Action**
	Interpretations/Indicators/ Targets Approval:	
	Monitoring Progress:	

Disposition of the Board:

Disposition of the Board		
Type of Report	**Yes/no**	
Interpretation/ Indicators/Targets		Interpretations are reasonable
		Exception(s) noted:
		Indicators are reasonable
		Exception(s) noted:
		Date for Re-monitoring:
		Targets are reasonable
		Exception(s) noted:
		Date for Re-monitoring:
Reasonable Progress		Reasonable progress has been made
		Exceptions(s) noted:
		Date for Re-monitoring:

Summary statement/motion of the board on each report:

Summary Statements
Interpretation/Indicator/Target Approval:

Judgment of Reasonable Progress:
Date: ______________________
CEO: ______________________
Chair: ______________________

Appendix B includes a compilation of several Results reports from a variety of organizations, all worthy of study. Readers should keep in mind that these are *samples,* and not intended to be examples of perfect monitoring reports. In the "Author's Notes," we point out what we consider to be some good features of the reports, as well as some suggestions to strengthen them.

Questions for Thought

1. How does your board now judge whether your organization is succeeding in meeting its outcome expectations?
2. What percentage of its time does your board now spend doing that work?
3. Would your board and CEO agree that progress toward achieving Results should be the dominant expectation of the board and the primary obligation of the CEO?

FAQs

Q: Does every Result policy need to be monitored every year?
A: Not necessarily, but unless there is a compelling case for not doing so, it is an advisable practice. The board establishes the frequency for monitoring based on many factors, including the availability of reliable and valid data, longitudinal targets, resources, and others. The board always controls the monitoring schedule.

Q: Who actually presents these Results reports? The CEO, or key staff members?

A: The CEO often designates staff members who have the authority and expertise in specific areas to draft the report and present it. The CEO should "tee up" the report and respond to any board questions. As the board's only employee, the CEO must take responsibility for the contents and presentation of any Results report.

Q: If the board decides that the report failed to demonstrate reasonable progress in one area, does that automatically throw the entire report into "unreasonable progress" status?

A: No. The board must apply the reasonable person standard and judge how significant the exception is to the whole. If the board concludes that every part of the Results policy is shown to be making reasonable progress with one exception, the overall assessment of progress would be "reasonable progress, with the exception of . . ."

Chapter 6

CEO Evaluation

> The Board considers CEO performance to be identical to organizational performance. Organizational accomplishment of the Board's Results policies and operation according to the values expressed in the Board's Operational Expectations policies will be considered successful CEO performance. These two components define the CEO's job responsibilities, and are the basis for the CEO's performance evaluation. (Coherent Governance Policy Template BCR.5)

The above policy statement is extracted from Coherent Governance® templates, and is very consistent with policy language found in most Policy Governance® manuals. It represents one of the fundamental and most significant concepts of both models: the performance of the organization and the performance of the CEO are identical. Stated simply, as goes the organization, so goes the CEO.

The previous two chapters in this book dealt with the board's monitoring role for both Operational Expectations and Results policies. As we will see in chapter 8, the board will develop an annual work plan that schedules the formal monitoring of the policies in these two categories throughout the year. As the board monitors R and OE policies, it is making judgments about the organization's reasonable progress toward achieving the Results, and its satisfaction with the organization's operational performance against the standards set by the OE policies.

As the board makes these judgments about the organization's performance, it also is building a portfolio of CEO performance. At the end of the complete monitoring cycle, these judgments of organizational performance will be "transferred" to the CEO, which serves to link the two together—as the above policy suggests.

This process is a dramatic departure from the methods most boards use to evaluate their CEOs. As a result of our combined sixty-plus years of working with boards, one startling fact has become clear: Most boards have no idea how to meaningfully evaluate their CEOs. From our experience, let us share the norm, rather than the exception, about how boards approach the process.

At the eleventh hour, a board president may call for help in a scramble to find a generic evaluation document to use for the CEO's evaluation, with no forethought about what that evaluation is intended to measure. In evaluation discussion sessions, members might contribute their personal feelings, biases, and reactions to how the CEO handled the latest challenge—or perhaps mishandled it, coloring a year's worth of work. Often the information discussed and documented as "evaluative" has little or no connection to the CEO's or the organization's actual performance.

As individual board members struggle with how to approach the task of CEO evaluation, they sometimes adopt opinions ranging from "*no one deserves an A*" to "*an evaluation isn't the time to criticize—look how hard s/he has been working.*" This retrospective would be remiss if it didn't also include reference to evaluations characterized by such personal attitudes ranging from *the CEO can do no wrong*, to the opposite, *the CEO can do nothing right.*

Quite obviously, neither mindset is commendable. Many times, given the difficulty of conducting evaluations that all parties find meaningful, boards skip the process altogether.

A MEANINGFUL EVALUATION PROCESS

The concept of linking organizational performance with CEO performance, as defined in the Results and Operational Expectations policies, means that if the organization's owners and clients realize the benefits the board said they should, and if the organization operates within the values of the board's Operational Expectations policies, the CEO has done the job he or she was hired to do.

If the board means what it has said in policy, these are the only criteria on which the CEO will be evaluated.

Actually, the process of CEO evaluation no longer is a one-time event, but rather an ongoing, continuous process. Each time the board monitors one of the Results or the OE policies, it is building a portion of the CEO's annual performance evaluation. The board is, in fact, creating a performance portfolio that at a defined point later in the year will become the basis for the CEO's summative evaluation.

When the scheduled time for the summative evaluation appears on the board's annual work plan, the compilation of board judgments on each report is reviewed. Let us point out here the invaluable role to be played by an assistant to the board who compiles each monitoring report and maintains records of board action to be used for this summative evaluation purpose.

The board president facilitates the board discussion and drafts a summary evaluation document for board approval based upon the monitoring record compiled throughout the year. The board's summative evaluation of the CEO could be no more than two or three pages of narrative comment, all based on the record generated by ongoing Results and Operational Expectations monitoring.

This illustrates why the OE and R monitoring process is so crucial to the overall effectiveness of the board's movement into Coherent Governance®. If the board neglects to do this job very well, it has, in fact, given away control of the organization. But if the board performs the monitoring role efficiently and effectively, it assumes a far greater degree of control than any "traditional" governing method would permit. And it assigns a greater degree of accountability than it ever thought possible.

Let us repeat here that from a technical standpoint, the regular and systematic monitoring of the Results and Operational Expectations policies are occasions for the board to assess how well the *organization*—not the CEO—is performing. At the point of the summative evaluation of the CEO, this record of organizational performance is transferred to the CEO, at which time the monitoring results become personal, not organizational. This subtle but important distinction prevents the monthly—and sometimes public—evaluation of the CEO.

Let us emphasize an important point about the board's summarizing the year's monitoring data. If the board has anything to say about exceptional organizational performance, either good or bad, the time to say it is when the relevant policy is being monitored. If the board has gone through a full year of monitoring the Results and Operational Expectations policies and has said nothing about a particular concern, it is unfair to inject any such unstated concerns during the summative evaluation process.

The purpose of the summative evaluation is to *summarize*, to draw conclusions from the work that has been done during the complete R and OE monitoring cycle. If the board has concerns about the maintenance of its facilities, for example, it should make a compliance judgment when the facilities OE policy is monitored, not inject such a concern after the fact.

On the other side of that same coin, if the board recognizes extraordinary performance and feels the need to offer commendation for it, that decision should be made when the relevant policy is monitored. Such action and the record of it provide the basis for the board's summative decision-making when the year's performance record is being used to evaluate the CEO's performance.

Of course, CEOs tend to accept, with gratitude, commendation whenever and however it is offered, whether the board made such a decision when the policy was being monitored or not. Nevertheless, in order to build a system that is based on consistency and reliability, the board is encouraged to develop the habit of assessing organizational performance very thoroughly and fairly when it is time to do so. Then, the board uses the record of its actions as the complete basis for summative CEO evaluation.

The CEO evaluation samples that follow are actual performance summations developed by different school boards following their annual review of organizational performance. They are based on compiled monitoring reports. The first sample starts with a cover letter (which is an executive summary) to the CEO that also includes his contract extension and performance pay, all based on the evaluation.

Date

RE: Superintendent's Performance Evaluation

The Board of Trustees met with you on (date), to conduct your annual performance evaluation as required by your employment contract with the Board of Trustees. As a result of the evaluation and the board's review of your monitoring reports during the past year, the board finds that the organization, and consequently you, have achieved reasonable progress on the Results related to Essential Skills, Responsible Citizenship, and, with exception, on Academic Achievement.

With respect to your performance on achieving compliance with the Operational Expectations the board has set for you, the board finds that you are in compliance regarding your performance on OE-1, Global Operational Expectation; OE-2, Instructional Program; OE-3, Treatment of Students and their Families; OE-4, Treatment of Staff; and OE-9, Compensation and Benefits. You are in compliance with commendations regarding your performance on OE-7, Emergency Superintendent Succession and OE-10, Communication and Support to the Board.

Regarding your performance on OE-5, Financial Planning/Budgeting, on the monitoring date of ______, you were in compliance with commendations; on the monitoring dates of ______, and ______, you were in compliance. Regarding your performance on OE-6, Financial Condition and Activities, on the monitoring dates of ______, and ______, you were in compliance; on the monitoring date of ______, you were in compliance with exception. Regarding your performance on OE-8, Asset Protection, on the monitoring date of

______, the board found you to be in compliance with exception; and on the monitoring date of ______, the board found you to be in compliance.

The board determined that your performance is satisfactory for the purpose of approving the percentage increase in compensation provided in addendum #2 to your employment contract.

Finally, the board voted to modify your employment contract to amend paragraph 3, Term, to extend your contract term from ______, to ______, as reflected in the attached Superintendent Contract Addendum #5.

We look forward to meeting with you before ______, for the purpose of the board's dialog with you to discuss your performance in relation to the Performance Evaluation document.

Sincerely,

President

B/CR-5

Policy Type: Board CEO Relationship
Annual Summative Evaluation of Superintendent
Date

Executive Summary

The board is pleased with the district's performance for the academic year (date). The superintendent's leadership during a time of higher academic standards and an uncertain financial future for public education is commendable.

The board recognizes that the superintendent's strengths have led to advancement on multiple fronts, including:

- Progress in academic achievement (R-2)
- Establishment of the Teacher Compensation Working Group (OE-5)
- Preparation of the 2004 Bond Package (OE-16)
- Initial High School Redesign efforts (R-3)
- Leadership/community visibility for public education and school finance (OE-10)

However, the district still faces significant challenges:

- Acceleration of progress toward elimination of the achievement gap, particularly compared to peer school districts (R-2)

- Effectiveness of middle schools preparing students for the rigor of H.S. (R-2)
- Implementation of the next phase of the High School Redesign Initiative (R-3)
- Improvement of customer service and treatment of stakeholders (OE-3)

The board looks forward to another year of progress and is confident that the superintendent will continue to build on these strengths and will address the challenges identified in this appraisal.

Results Monitoring

Based upon the Results information provided, the board reaches the following conclusions relative to the superintendent's performance.

R-2 Academic Achievement

The board appreciates the significant gains made in the area of writing, the overall number of students passing state tests, the number of campuses recognized for Gold Performance, and greater gains made by our district as compared to relative gains statewide.

However, the district needs to focus on academic achievement for all student groups in math and science. African American student achievement still lags behind too many subgroups, including economically disadvantaged and English language learners. The board's expectation is that math and science scores will improve and that African American students will exceed or match the state average at both the passing and the commended level.

The board is pleased with the additional focus on English language learners, bilingual education, and new initiatives for the district's growing populations of immigrant students, including the International High School at ______. However, the district's Spanish test takers still lag behind the State's Spanish test takers. Hispanic students, who comprise over 55 percent of enrollment, are not succeeding at the same levels as Hispanic students statewide. The board's expectation is that Hispanic students will exceed or match the state average at both the passing and the commended level.

Our district must increase the number and percentage of students achieving at the commended level across all ethnic groups and income levels. The board's expectation is that students will match or exceed the state average for commended achievement in (date).

R-3 College and Career

The superintendent is to be commended for the initial steps to improve the high school experience for students based on the principles of rigor, relevance, relationships and results. The district continues to build its strong partnership with our community college, and has increased the number of students graduating under the Recommended High School Plan. However, the district must accelerate its high school redesign efforts over the next twelve months and move from planning into action, including a meaningful public engagement process.

The district's focus on high schools cannot ignore the significant need to dramatically improve and upgrade the district's middle schools, especially in math and science.

R-7 Health and Safety

The board commends the Superintendent for progress in ensuring that more students understand the principles and practice of a healthy, active lifestyle, and his strong steps to provide better choices of nutritious food. However, the district must address the challenges of high school students' illegal use of drugs and alcohol. The board expects the superintendent to present analysis of the Signature Science Operational Assessment of the city police department, and after receiving direction from the board, implement the appropriate and necessary recommendations for improving campus safety and security.

Results: Strengths

R-2 Academic Achievement

- Improvement in performance in writing on state tests
- Greater overall district gains made by the district than statewide
- Increased percentages of students passing
- Number of campuses cited for Gold Performance acknowledgment
- Focus on bilingual education/creation of the international school

R-3 College and Career

- Establishment of community college and district partnership
- Increased number of students who graduated under RHSP
- Continued improvement in the completion rate and the four-year graduation rate

R-7 Health and Safety

- Strong leadership in health, nutrition and fitness

Results: Areas of Focus

R-2 Academic Achievement

- Need to improve academic achievement of all student groups with a focus on math and science

- African American student achievement lags behind too many student subgroups, including economically disadvantaged and English language learners
- Students lag behind the state average for all subgroups in achieving commended status
- Spanish test takers lag behind the state average for Spanish test takers

R-3 College and Career

- Implementation of High School Redesign and meaningful public engagement
- Improvement on middle school state tests performance and campus Gold Performance representation across the district

R-7 Health and Safety

- Analysis and implementation of Police Department Audit
- Increased enforcement of drug and alcohol violations at campuses

Operational Expectations

Based upon the Operational Expectations information provided, the board reaches the following conclusions relative to the superintendent's performance:

The board is pleased with the superintendent's continued progress in addressing Operational Expectations as established through board policy. Of particular note is the high compliance rating reached throughout this evaluation period. The superintendent is to be commended on the stronger human resource practices implemented, continued emphasis on financial stability, his commitment to district wide curriculum alignment, and overall better communication with the board, staff, and stakeholders. The superintendent has also maintained a strong and positive visible presence in the community. While much success has been realized, there are some areas of focus the board wishes to emphasize, that if addressed, will bring about even better outcomes for the district.

Operational Expectations: Strengths

- Attained 90 percent full compliance on OE policies
- Implemented district wide curriculum alignment (OE 12)
- Developed long term facilities plan in preparation of the Bond (OE 16)
- Created stronger human resources support (OE 5)
- Formation of the Teacher Compensation Working Group
- Improved teacher evaluation process

- Attained highest number of National Board Certified Teachers in state
- Achieved 100 percent administrative appraisals and 99.7 percent teacher appraisals
- Continued outstanding financial viability (OE 7)
- Maintained strong budget management and bond rating
- Allocated needed resources to support Results policies
- Established better communication (OE 10)
- Improved communication between board and superintendent
- Broadened communication efforts within the district and external audiences

Operational Expectations: Areas of Focus

- Respectful treatment of stakeholders at all levels throughout the district (OE 3)
- Expectation should be included in principal evaluation
- Acknowldgment of parents and community members as partners
- Expand circle of valued voices to deepen appreciation of diverse needs and outcomes of the community (OE 10)
- Follow-up to issues raised with the study on high schools (OE 4)
- Create and maintain an effective facilities data base with public access to nonclassified information of campus data (OE 16)
- Create a stronger organizational culture that encourages creative thinking and values open and honest communication (OE 4)

Signed: ____________ Board President Date: ______________

Signed: ____________ Superintendent Date: ______________

The second sample is very similar, although a bit more condensed. Both samples may be considered as examples of formats to help the board organize its approach and evaluative comments.

For obvious reasons, we have omitted any identifying information.

Summative Performance Evaluation of CEO
School District Board of Education

Date

The members of the Board of Education commend your invaluable leadership to the school district and to the Board of Education during the past year. We look forward to your continuing service to this board and community.

We have committed to evaluating our superintendent based on our Operational Expectations and reasonable progress on our Results policies.

Operational Expectations

Special commendation is extended for your exceptional successes in the following areas:

1. OE-, 5, 6, 7: Budget/Financial Administration/Asset Protection
   You have a very competent administrator in ______ and his staff who are worthy of commendation. Under your leadership, they focus on funding student achievement priorities; nurturing an open and transparent relationship with our community members and the teachers' union; present the budget in a way that is understandable to the board and citizens. Particularly noteworthy is the fact that your prudent conservation of reserves avoided any staff layoffs and built trust with staff and union.

2 OE-10: Instructional Program
   You have successfully addressed different learning styles and needs by concentrating on students with special disabilities and English language learners. We will look forward to data that affirms your approach and results in a narrowing of the achievement gap of these subgroups. We are impressed with the use of technology; getting tools in the hands of students and staff that are required for modern teaching and learning.
   The recent hire of ______with her beliefs, practices and expectations has supported your focus, and ours, on high student achievement for all students.

3. OE-11: Student Discipline
   Your effort and that of ______ and his staff, to address the hearings on student expulsions has produced a more expedient process for students and their families.

4. OE-4: Personnel Administration
   The board recognizes a credible relationship that has been developed with the teachers' union. We believe the union trusts the values and actions of the board and administration due in no small part to your practice of excellent communication, transparency and respect.

In addition, there is an improved relationship between the district office and school sites by fostering collaboration and an elevated focus on student achievement.

5. OE-8: Communication with the Board
   We appreciate your providing an open line of communication with the board and supporting our continuing education. In particular, we note your focus on twenty-first-century skills.

6. OE-9: Communications with the Public
   The board recognizes the effort to develop community awareness and support for our district. You have done an excellent job covering the community with speeches and appearances in order to build support.
   We are concerned that you overextend yourself. We encourage you to be your own time steward and be wary of excessive, ongoing commitments at the expense of your personal well-being.
   We ask that you address our values in OE-3 regarding accessibility and responsiveness of staff to vendors and others.

Results for Student Achievement

We commend you for the level of reasonable progress being achieved towards our defined Academic, Citizenship, and Personal Development Results. Given our diverse student population, it is a challenge to meet the needs of all children and move them to and beyond proficiency. We agree that the ELL and special disabilities students need focused attention on student achievement.

R.1 Mission
Student progress is predicated upon attendance. We commend you for actively seeking and improving the student attendance rate, which is a cumulative measure of your leadership, initiatives and programs.
The board encourages emphasis on raising the high school graduation rate. We need consistency and accuracy on reporting this data.

R.2 Students will be literate. This shall be the district's top priority.
Conclusion on 2.1–2.4: Reasonable Progress with the exception of ELL and special disabilities students.

2.1 Achieve proficiency in English
2.2 Read at grade level
2.4 Write clearly and effectively for a stated purpose.

Conclusion on 2.5: Reasonable Progress

2.5 Students will use technology to gain, analyze and evaluate information.

Conclusion on 2.6: Reasonable progress

2.6 Students will use the arts as a creative and emotional outlet to enhance academic success and personal fulfillment

Conclusion on 2.7: Reasonable progress toward achieving the desired results in mathematics and science. Reasonable progress with the exception of history/social science

2.7 Students will meet or exceed state standards in core academic disciplines

R.3 Students will acquire the skills and knowledge to actively lead, serve and contribute to their communities, make informed life choices and exhibit the habits and behaviors to achieve productive, healthy and balanced lives.

Conclusion: Reasonable progress

Results: Process Improvement

1. We need a consistent format for the Results reports with clear statements of:

   a. Reasonable interpretation
   b. Established indicators
   c. Targets for student achievement (disaggregated)
   d. Data clearly presented and analyzed
   e. Assertion of progress and exceptions

2. Adjust targets to build on prior levels of achievement. Current performance in some areas is considerably higher than targets. These targets would not be acceptable next year.
3. Again, a consistent and clear cover document for each report capturing the vote of the board with our official board decision on progress.

Additionally, the board will schedule a work session to discuss the level of challenge being offered to our higher achieving students.

Questions for Thought

1. How does your board now conduct CEO evaluations?
2. Are they based on a well-defined set of expectations that includes both operational and results performance?
3. Does your board now make decisions—through the approval process or otherwise—for which the CEO ultimately is held accountable?

FAQs

Q: Is it advisable to conduct a board self-assessment prior to conducting the CEO's summative evaluation?

A: Absolutely! Has the board lived up to its commitments, those expressed in both the GC and BCR policies? Many of them affect the CEO's job. The board must do its job well before attempting to assess CEO performance against board expectations.

Q: Does a summative evaluation of the CEO have any real meaning? If the board has been doing its job of OE and R monitoring throughout the year, isn't this just an arcane formality?

A: The summative CEO evaluation allows the board to draw summary judgment. As a result of the year's monitoring experience, what becomes clear to the board? What performance areas are worthy of commendation? What areas become apparent as priorities for the next operational cycle? What noteworthy successes should drive decisions about performance-based compensation? The summative evaluation is the vehicle the board uses to transfer judgments of district performance to the CEO personally. It cannot be neglected.

Q: Should the CEO provide a summary self-assessment?

A: Such a self-assessment can be useful, but it should not be substituted for the board's own deliberations and judgments, based upon the performance record that has been compiled throughout the monitoring period.

Chapter 7

Stakeholder Dialog

If you are a publicly elected board member, chances are good that you "linked" fairly effectively with your ownership when you were campaigning for election. Or even after the election, the board very likely "linked" with the owners when it needed votes for new taxes or support for some other matter important to the organization.

But absent the urgent need for votes, how closely linked is the board to the people who own the organization? How proactively does the board seek continuing, meaningful dialog with those owners?

Once in office, how do board members connect with the people they serve, lead, and represent—not just as individuals, but as a whole board? In particular, how do individuals broaden their governing obligation to understand and serve *all* the owners as a means to better understand the needs of the entire organization?

In the board's new job description (GC-3), one of the first roles is the board's commitment to engage in ongoing, proactive linkage with the owners and stakeholders. This means that the board must develop a very deliberate, structured plan for establishing and executing that kind of communication.

Throughout this chapter we will refer to this role as *stakeholder dialog*, or *dialog*. Some boards label the effort *linkage,* or *public engagement*, or some other such term. We will use *dialog* as a term that captures the role, realizing that your board may attach a different label to it.

It should be emphasized that the dialog role is a *board* responsibility, not a board *member* responsibility. Individual members have and will continue to have personal relationships with people both inside and outside the organization, and they will talk with them on occasion. This is not *dialog* as defined in board policy. The dialog function is a whole-board function, based on strategies defined by the board. This does not necessarily mean that every member must participate in every dialog session, as we will discuss later in this chapter, but it does mean that fulfillment of the dialog role is not an individual responsibility.

DIALOG WITH WHOM?

A very important point needs to be made here. Some consultants and writers believe it the board's obligation to dialog only with their owners, not those who have different "stakeholder" roles with the organization. Of course, depending on the type of organization the board serves, those could be, at least in large measure, the same people. In a voluntary membership organization, for example, the owners and clients virtually are the same people, although some segments of the ownership can take on a narrower role when they have a particular need or desire not shared by the entire ownership.

It is our belief that boards owe singular loyalty to their owners—the public, in the case of a publicly elected board—but they can benefit from structured dialog with groups other than their owners. They can build stronger understanding of and advocacy for the organization if they develop relationships with clients and customers, for example, and with a range of stakeholder groups that have varying relationships with the organization.

In the case of public school boards, dialog could include students, for example. On occasion, it even could include selected employee groups, if there is good reason, provided such interactions are with the concurrence of the CEO and are carefully structured in order to avoid any role confusion or crossing of lines. If the board does interact with employee groups, there must be clear understanding of the purpose, and the discussion must be structured in such a way that it is constructive and focused on the board's topic, and not allowed to become a gripe session.

We will acknowledge that most of the board's dialog focus should be on key individuals and groups who comprise the ownership. Employees and other such "inside" groups usually have ways of conveying information to the board. It is the ownership to whom the board ultimately is accountable, and there should be no question about the identity of that ownership.

The primary objective of the dialog role is to provide a means for the board to better understand the needs and expectations of the owners, as seen through their eyes, in order to prepare the board to make the best decisions in its governing role. A second objective is to allow the board to share with the owners and stakeholders its vision for organizational performance as a means to build stronger support for where the organization is headed.

The challenge to build an effective dialog plan for the board can seem formidable. If the organization is substantially "self-contained" (a volunteer membership organization, for example), meaningful engagement with the membership may be a relatively easy thing to do. But if the organization is a public school district, whose owners include everyone who lives within the borders of the district, the task is considerably more difficult.

But regardless of the nature of the organization's ownership, effectively performing this role is critical if the board is to:

- Build mutually supportive relationships between the board and its owners and stakeholders;
- Inform the board about the expectations of the owners;
- Translate the owners' expectations into policies;
- Create understanding among the ownership about the board's Results.

PROCEDURALLY, HOW DOES A BOARD GO ABOUT CREATING A DIALOG PLAN?

There are multiple ways for boards to develop a plan for communicating with their stakeholders. A number of variables must be considered, including the size and complexity of the organization and its ownership; the nature of the organization in terms of its mission and the definition of its overall purpose; and the capacity of the organization and the board to try some sophisticated processes.

Some fundamental dialog concepts do apply to all organizations, however.

For the first dialog sessions, we recommend focusing all of your efforts on Results. *Walk the talk* about the purpose of the organization with a laser focus on the benefits to be realized by those your organization exists to serve.

We suggested in chapter 2 that the board's early implementation of Coherent Governance® should be launched with as little fanfare as possible in order to avoid making your new venture a target. Some of what we suggest here may sound contradictory, but it need not be.

There are critical individuals and groups of your organization's owners and stakeholders who will need to understand your shift of focus in order for them to become advocates for your venture. Bring them into the loop early by establishing solid two-way discussions with them.

Once you have adopted your policies and revised your board meeting agendas to redirect the board's dominant attention to Results, consider some of the following strategies. They are designed to focus staff and the owners, with the board, on increased achievement of Results. The list includes a variety of options to consider, based on the type of organization your board leads.

Invite targeted groups of the ownership to meet with the board. People learn by doing and engaging. You have the opportunity to brief them about the board's renewed focus on Results and your need to involve and partner with them.

Meet with the local newspaper editorial staff. If you are a public organization, talk with local media about your new focus. Ask them to watch for the increased focus your board and organization will be demonstrating on the Results. Invite them to attend a board meeting where you are working on a Results policy.

Meet with your clients. We recommend representative discussions across the spectrum of groups served by your organization. If you are in the business of elder care, talk with your seniors and their family members. If you are a school district, student groups are enlightening—and refreshing in their honesty. If you are an insurance pool, pool participants will have an avid interest in your identified Results. The members of a voluntary membership organization will be anxious to talk about your new focus on what membership dues are purchasing.

Meet with any active volunteer groups. Involved advocates can serve as great opinion leaders with others for getting out the word that things are indeed changing. These groups can have a meaningful role in influencing and shaping broader owner opinion and encouraging support. Consider establishing a Key Communicator Network of opinion leaders for ongoing communication. In appendix C, we include an outline for starting such a network and the results of one organization's Key Communicator activities.

Meet with various community organizations. You will know which ones exercise influence and sway opinion: business and civic associations, Rotary Club, Elks Club, Cattlemen's Association, Chamber of Commerce, League of Women Voters, and so forth. Schedule a session for a board member to provide an overview of your new venture and its dominant focus on Results.

Conduct surveys. Lay the groundwork for change by conducting surveys, via the web, paper or telephone, on what your owners expect. By asking their opinion, they become part of the solution and will be waiting for further information and perhaps involvement.

Some boards hire public relations specialists to assist them in developing a plan for communicating with various stakeholder groups. Some organizations have communications experts on staff assigned the duty of supporting the board in its communication efforts. Other boards form a "Communications/Dialog Committee" to formulate a plan to recommend to the board. We have no specific preference for where support should come from, but in larger or more complex organizations, the board will need support from some such source.

As we have said before, there is no one way to do this work—just do it! Resources are available to help you define what works best for you, initially and over time.

FUNDAMENTAL TWO-WAY DIALOG CONCEPTS

Establishing a conversation of give-and-take is the beginning of a meaningful relationship between the board and its owners. This is always best done face-to-face, where the board can watch faces and body language, ask follow-up and probing questions, and allow diverse members of the group to hear feedback that may be diametrically opposite to their own opinion. They hear and hopefully appreciate the challenge posed by this diversity as you perform your governing role.

FOCUS GROUPS

We recommend focus groups as one strategy for linking with your owners and stakeholders in order to achieve the outcomes that we discussed above. The primary purpose of engaging in a focus group dialog discussion is to share information about board work and to gather information from the group about issues of concern to the board. The focus group format, which features a hand-selected group of ten to twelve individuals representing an identified segment of your ownership, is good for depth of discussion about a few topics. It is not as useful if the board is interested in a broader sounding of opinions about many topics.

The focus group is not intended to provide an opportunity for the group to unload its issues on the board. There are ample opportunities for the latter to be accomplished without allowing a very positive, informative conversation to degenerate into a gripe session.

- *The board should determine the major components for the focus group session,* including:
  - identification of the topic;
  - identification of, and invitation to, participants;
  - location and timing;
  - the questions to be asked;
  - welcoming, conducting, and ending the meeting;
  - ensuring that all appropriate physical arrangements are made;
  - ensuring that participants receive appropriate follow-up.
- *Topics for focus group conversations primarily should be about the board's Results policies.* In our experience, many participants will want to steer the

discussion toward operations, and in fact there may be instances when the board will want to discuss some operational concern. But Results should be the centerpiece of the board's work, and therefore should be the normal topic of focus group discussions.

- In determining individuals or groups for invitations, *the board should decide whose opinions would be informative to the board.* Any people who are invited should receive personal written invitations *from the board (not staff; this is board work)* with a response card attached.

Some boards attach a list of all people who have been invited in order to show each invitee that he or she is among a select group and will be missed i.' s/he fails to accept. Appropriate follow-up via telephone also may be necessary.

- *Limit the number of questions to three or four.* This number of questions should allow for reasonable give-and-take and for follow-up, probing questions to be asked. We cannot overstate the importance of carefully constructed questions. Good questions lead to good answers.
- If the board decides to hold focus group conversations with several small groups on the same topic, *ask the same questions of each group.* This allows the board to compare what it has heard from each group and to see similarities as well as differences.
- *After each session, quickly debrief on what you have heard.* After having heard from a number of groups, the board should schedule a debriefing session to allow it to get a broader picture, an overview, and decide if further action or policy work is needed.
- *Settle on a schedule that requires minimal additional work for members.* If dialog meetings can be appended to the regular board meeting or to some other event, days and evenings can be saved.
- *Each dialog meeting should be around ninety minutes in length.* It is difficult to get much done in less than ninety minutes, and people are less productive if the meeting lasts longer than that. Start and end on time!

BEYOND FOCUS GROUPS

In considering dialog strategies, the board should decide whether it wants and needs small, informal give-and-take discussions with relatively small homogeneous groups (clergy, business interests, students, seniors, parents, etc.), or whether it wants to hear from larger, more diverse groups. This decision will depend on many factors, including the need to get broad input fast from many people as opposed to gathering more in-depth information from identifiable groups over a longer period of time.

As a rule, the full board participates in all dialog discussions, if possible. In some large organizations, it may be necessary, at least in part, to divide the load to get the job done. However, when less than the full board hears what is being said, something is lost when the discussion is translated to the whole board.

Some boards choose to divide into groups to conduct dialog discussions because of the size and complexity of the organization or community of owners the board serves. In such cases, we always recommend that at least two members participate in each meeting. This offers the advantage of at least two perspectives about what was heard as well as lightening the load for any one member.

Of course, the strategies for meaningful dialogs are limitless. In addition to focus group–type discussions with small groups, boards very effectively have used such strategies as:

- "town hall"–type meetings in which everyone with a stake in the organization is invited
- paper surveys
- electronic surveys (via Internet and otherwise)
- discussion sessions in the community-of-owners sub-areas
- "public engagement" sessions facilitated by neutral parties
- study circles—an innovative approach for solving conflicts (www.studycircles.org)
- "key communicator" discussions with a pre-identified group of opinion leaders
- owner meetings with expert speakers on specific topics

The task is to identify strategies that make sense to the board, given the nature and complexity of the organization and its ownership.

As we have already mentioned, whatever strategies the board selects, it will need adequate support to make the dialog function successful. This support may not necessarily require added staff, but from some source—existing staff, volunteer help, board committees, or a combination of all—there is some detailed support work to be performed. Putting that element in place early will serve the board well when the dialog work begins.

A TEMPLATE: HOW TO GET STARTED

The organized, full-board focus on continuing interaction with the owners and stakeholders very likely is work the board never has done before. So just how does a board, especially one with limited support resources, shift its attention to the task and start performing the role with some degree of proficiency?

Exhibit 7.1 is a "fill-in-the-blank" template for creating a communication plan for the board's interaction with its owners and stakeholders. The full board makes the final decision about all the components, including meeting format, dates, people to be involved, the questions to be asked, and other, related details.

EXHIBIT 7.1

Stakeholder Dialog Template

What? Who? Where? When? How?	A board committee develops a proposed plan and recommends to the board.
What topic(s) do we want to discuss?	A. B. C.
With whom will we meet?	A. B. C. D.
Who meets with them?	A. B. C. D.
Where do we meet?	A. B. C.
When do we meet?	A. B.
What linkage strategy do we want to use?	

What questions will we ask?	1. 2. 3. 4.

Fairfax County School Board Linkage Plan

The Fairfax, Virginia School Board used this template some years ago to develop its initial dialog plan. Exhibit 7.2 represents that board's completed document.

EXHIBIT 7.2

FCPS Community Conversations

What? Who? Where? When? How?	Board committee makes initial plans to recommend to the board.
What topic(s) do we want to discuss?	A. Broad overview: Beliefs, Vision, Mission B. Major focus: Student achievement goals • Valuable enough to be actionable? • Perceptions? • Impact?
How and with whom do we meet? Index: D = district dialog F = focus group K = key communicators C = community O = other S = survey L = liaison	• Existing advisory groups • Cultural groups (F) • Class of 2005 (F) • Leadership team (F) • Current students (F) • Faith-based community (K,F) • Civic/homeowner assns. (D,K) • Business community (F,K) • Community leaders (K) • Parents (D) • Senior citizens/retirees (F,K) • Principal assns. (S) • Teachers and employees (S) • Legislators (O)

Who on board meets with them?	• Board of Supervisors (O) • Focus Groups: significant number of members (4-6) • District Dialog: host district member plus at least one other member • Key Communicators: entire BOE • Community Forum: entire BOE • Other: entire BOE • Advisory Board Liaisons: appointed member plus one
Where do we meet?	A. Chairman and superintendent will devise a method/process for logistics B. The board will meet where it is most convenient for the invitees
How do we meet? Linkage strategies to consider, both short and long term.	*Focus Groups* (twelve to fifteen people representing defined group) *District Dialog* (come one–come all meeting in member districts; involves at least host-member and one or more other members) *Key Communicators* (continuing group of forty to fifty key opinion leaders from throughout county; meet quarterly for two-way conversation with entire board) *Community Forum* (come one–come all meeting; initial full-group presentation, then facilitated subgroups with all members facilitating)
When do we meet?	• Between now and May • June product delivery • Weekdays • District dialog—evenings • Focus groups—dependent on group • Keep under 2 hours (7–9 or 6–8 PM) • Key Communicators: bkfst or lunch

What questions do we ask?	1. What expectations do you have of a graduate of our school system? In other words, what should they be prepared to do? 2. Do you believe these goals will accomplish those expectations? • Are they appropriate and relevant? • Are they ambitious enough? • Are they too ambitious? 3. How will we be able to determine whether students achieve their potential? 4. The board has identified what it considers to be essential life skills. Are there other specific skills you would add to this goal? 5. How would students demonstrate that they are productive citizens?
During and After Linkage Sessions: Synthesizing Process	• Provide a recorder for each meeting. • Record either on flip chart or laptop/ overhead (or both) • Use a consistent format for presentation of meeting outcomes (Q&A) • Board members debrief with each other directly after each meeting; information will be captured electronically by staff and then be shared with the rest of the board members in an executive summary format consistently through out the entire process • Summary response to each question • Debriefing summary • Individual notes • Staff members will synthesize responses as the process continues, noting trends and themes

Next Steps	• Craft an invitation that attracts attendees. Must be compelling. • Develop exit survey. • Identify and invite individuals to key focus groups. • Notify community about meetings. (Channel 21, newspapers, KIT, PTA newsletters, civic assns, churches, pyramid/school newsletters) • Meeting participants sign-in sheets with email address for follow up. • Follow up: "Thanks for coming; here's what we heard; here's what we're going to do with the information." • Notify all participants when the synthesized goals are completed. • Publish final product for the world, needs to be translated. (same outlets as above)

Fairfax County School Board Exit Questionnaire of Focus Group Participants

To supplement the information received by the Fairfax board during the several focus group discussions, the board also invited each participant to complete a written questionnaire. The information that the board collected from the written responses was compiled and summarized, along with the summarized results of the focus group discussions.

Fairfax County Public Schools Exit Survey

As your elected board members, we are very anxious to connect with all of our citizens as you entrust us to represent your needs and to provide governance leadership at the school district level.

We feel a vital need to work with you to focus on and increase the level of achievement with all of our students in this county.

Would you take a few moments and respond to the questions we are asking below? Your insight and feedback will be summarized with the rest of the surveys we collect and then the results shared with you at the follow up Forum meeting this fall. We will also share with you our responses and plan of action at that time!

1. The goals are in the school board's priority order; do you agree with that priority?
   Yes __
   No __
   If not, how would you prioritize them?
2. You have $10 total to spend; how would you allocate it among the three?
   Academic Achievement: $ __
   Life Skills: $ __
   Citizenship: $ __
3. What barriers exist to prevent our children from achieving these goals?
   a.
   b.
   c.
4. Have you felt listened to and had your values heard at this meeting?
   Yes __
   No __
5. Will you attend the follow up meeting in the fall to hear the results of all citizen feedback and board focus on student achievement goals?
   Yes __
   No __
6. What do you believe are the greatest issues challenging our district in working to improve achievement?
   a.
   b.
   c.
7. The board members are striving to work together with a diligent focus of our time and resources to meet the needs of *all* students, despite the many differences among our districts and community. What recommendations would you make to us to increase our effectiveness as a whole board?
   a.
   b.
   c.
8. Where do you receive your most reliable information from about the board and its work?
9. How would you prefer to receive information from your board member and the board? (Please circle your highest preference): newsletter website email regular meetings television other—please identify
10. What kind of information do you most want to hear about from your board member and board?

11. Would you attend a "district" meeting with your local school board member to find out more about district wide issues and to share your local insight and concerns?
    Yes __
    No __
12. What time of the day is best for you? Circle one:
    early morning   lunchtime   before dinner   early evening
13. We vitally are interested in increasing parental involvement with their children in the schools. Many different ideas are being tried across the nation. What do you believe our board could do at the policy level to encourage parents to be part of their children's school and overall education?
14. Please share any feedback you have on the beliefs, vision and mission that the school board has adopted:

Thank you for your time and interest!
Please return this form to the sign-in table where you entered the meeting.

Nikkei Concerns Community Linkages in Seattle, WA

Nikkei Concerns is a Seattle nonprofit organization that provides elder care services for members of the Japanese American community. The Board of Directors arranged for face-to-face discussions with important elements of its well-defined community in order to share with them the board's work in drafting Results policies. The board also solicited from the community groups their opinions about potential and significant long-term changes to maintain the organization's viability in that particular community.

Appendix C includes the questions the board posed to these owner groups, along with the board's facilitation copy *in italics*. We suggest the use of a recorder whose job includes writing verbatim responses on flipcharts for all participants to see and think about as participants respond. The Nikkei Concerns questions are good, but we recommend limiting the number of questions to four to six in order to allow for adequate follow-up questions and for balanced input among participants.

KEY COMMUNICATORS: STRATEGIC COMMUNICATIONS

We wrote earlier in this chapter about another dialog strategy, Key Communicators. A Key Communicator group simply is a selected group of "key" people in the community, or individuals who have some interest in the organization and its welfare. They are people who tend to have credibility within the broader community, people who command respect and attention when they speak or offer an opinion.

Key Communicator groups tend to be comprised of visible people in the community, including some people who may hold important positions. However, there well may be individuals in the community who do not carry impressive titles, but who nevertheless are opinion leaders among those with whom they interact.

Consider these possibilities: a former board member, a popular breakfast café manager, stylists at the local salon or barbershop. In selecting people to serve, the board should look beyond titles and positions, and determine the most listened-to people among various elements of the broader ownership.

To create such a group, the board identifies up to thirty or so people it considers to fit the qualification profile. Then the board invites them to meet periodically (perhaps quarterly) for information updates and to learn and to share information, both ways.

Since the Key Communicators strategy requires members to serve on an ongoing basis rather than one-time interaction with the board, the board will need to build into the process a bit more formality. This helps to assure that the group serves a contributing purpose and does not become, over time, a controlling body rather than a contributing one. We recommend that the board invite participants for a one-year term only. Some members could be asked to return for another year, if the board chooses, but we encourage the board to guard against creating lifetime appointments for this or any other group.

Appendix C includes a suggested process to activate a Key Communicators group as an ongoing communication strategy.

HOW ONE SCHOOL BOARD ENGAGED THE COMMUNITY TO DEFINE RESULTS

One proactive school board conducted a series of dialog sessions, which the board called "Voices to Vision." The board held meetings across its very large and diverse community, focusing on the board's newly developed Results policies.

The whole group process centered on gathering input from community members/owners about the importance of student citizenship and participants' willingness to help students become model citizens. The process yielded remarkably consistent results among respondents within each meeting and across the community.

Appendix C includes the abbreviated documents associated with this campaign, including the original Citizenship Result, the focus group agenda, and meeting protocols. The last document in the set includes the policy revisions that resulted from the feedback from the community-wide sessions.

(The extent to which this board chose to restate its Results expectations based on owner feedback may well exceed what most boards would find necessary and desirable. That isn't the point to showing it here. Our objective is to use this board's work as an example of how boards can use information to advance their own work, not to advocate for this degree of detail in policy development.)

HOW ONE SCHOOL BOARD PROACTIVELY RESPONDED TO CHALLENGE

Another school board was challenged with significant internal divisions, some very trying district-wide circumstances, as well as state-level political dynamics. The board determined the need to quickly engage with its owners about its new focus on Results and increased accountability of the superintendent.

In order to sustain members' focus and lead the community to support the board and school efforts, the board, with the aid of its director of communications, developed a comprehensive and strategic communication plan for the board's short-term use in dealing with the issue. It is the final detailed example we have included in appendix C. Note that the *Board Listening Campaign* focuses on the informal Key Communicators strategy.

STAKEHOLDER DIALOG: IN SUMMARY

It is apparent that developing an effective dialog plan for the governing board of a large and complex organization is a significant task for a part-time board of directors to undertake. If the organization is relatively small and "compact," the task may be much easier. But for the board of a larger organization with a broad ownership base, support and guidance from someone who understands the intricacies of effective communication will be invaluable.

Boards are encouraged to explore a variety of dialog strategies as they work with expert help and build a communication plan to meaningfully engage their stakeholders. This is hard work, but it can be some of the most important and rewarding work the board will do.

Questions for Thought

1. Does your board now have a plan to communicate with your owners?
2. When and how do you—as a full board—deliberately interact with the people the board serves and represents?
3. What is the difference between individual members' interacting with people within their own circles and the full board's role in owner interface?

FAQs

Q: If we have already determined the Results for the organization, what purpose is served by involving our owners and stakeholders in discussion about them?

A: Your owners deserve to know what you have established as expectations for organizational performance. Their understanding of your Results will either validate your assumptions or provide information for refining your policies. Any disagreement with your Results, priorities, or costs will provide the basis for more work and conversation, ultimately leading to even better definition of what benefits the organization is expected to deliver for whom, and at what cost.

Q: After initial conversation with owners about Results, what comes next?

A: Truth telling! What is the organization now doing well? Where do the board and organization need to focus? How can owners help? Remember, people want to be part of something larger than themselves.

Q: It sounds as if this communications effort requires more work of the board. Is it worth the time and money?

A: What are the consequences of not bringing your owners into their organization? Can you get too far ahead of their expectations? Can they rebel when one subgroup is getting more attention than others? Might they fail to understand why you need more fiscal resources? The price of not communicating can be greater than the cost of communicating.

Q: Isn't this something staff is better prepared to do than the board?
A: Being a trustee for the ownership means you are accountable to those you represent, lead, and serve. Accountability requires direct communication between those two parties. Your CEO does and will continue to have a strong role to play in communicating with various stakeholder groups, but the CEO wears a different hat and communicates for different purposes. The board simply has a job to do that only it can do.

Chapter 8

The Board's Annual Work Plan

Most boards have no idea what they will be working on from one meeting to the next. They have no defined schedule for their work, and consequently they tend to spend most of their time doing whatever someone else says they should do, or whatever feels right at the time.

An annual work plan is a built-in feature of your Coherent Governance® or Policy Governance® method of doing business. We have never worked with a board that, once acquainted with the idea of a work plan for a full year, ever abandoned that excellent tool for good governance.

Planning its own annual work empowers the board to exercise leadership for the organization, to regulate its workflow, and to demonstrate its accountability to the owners—all based on a logical, thoughtful sequence.

Every organization and work team performs better when it plans its work. The purpose of planning is to help the board move logically into the future, doing the things that the board thoughtfully has identified as its priority work. This deliberate and careful planning prevents the board from reacting to the crisis of the day, or equally misguided, spending time doing whatever the agenda has on it, regardless of the board's view of what is important.

The annual work plan is the basis for establishing each board meeting agenda. The board's scheduled actions and discussions are transferred at the designated time from the work plan to the regular board meeting agenda, and therefore define the board's ongoing work. The work plan allows the board to schedule its work in these important areas:

- GC monitoring
- B/CR monitoring
- OE monitoring

- Results monitoring and related work
- Stakeholder dialog
- Board development
- Any other tasks or events the board should plan its work around

The annual work plan offers the board an opportunity to assume responsibility for its own work and to anticipate thoughtfully the issues its meeting agendas should be built around. These are some of the questions that drive the scheduling of the work plan as the last step before adoption of the policies and venturing into this new world of governing:

1. When should the board self-assess? Does it want to do all GC and B/CR policy monitoring at one time during an annual retreat? Should the board divide the work into quarterly sessions? Would self-monitoring be done better in work sessions? Should monitoring be facilitated by a third party?
2. When should OE reports logically be presented in coordination with other functions of the organization, such as the financial audit?
3. When will data be available during the year that may drive the scheduling of Results monitoring reports? How can the board logically receive interpretations and indicators prior to monitoring progress? How much time will it take? A full meeting, or more than a single meeting? What activities should be scheduled within a regular meeting? Does the board need a special meeting?
4. What owner dialog sessions does the board want to schedule, and with whom? Will these be separate meetings, or coordinated with the existing meeting schedule?
5. What other commitments does the board have—conferences, conventions, audits, and so on?

The CEO and staff are well served by having ample lead time—sometimes a full year—to prepare for the dialog, deliberations, reports, and presentations the board has identified as important. Therefore, it becomes apparent that the annual board work plan is a tool not only to assist the board in scheduling its work, but also to help the staff organize its work in support of the board.

The annual work plan is not intended to be firmly implanted and unchangeable; it can and should be modified as circumstances and events require—but changed only by the board. It is the property of the board, not the CEO. If the CEO determines that some schedule change should occur, that change should be presented to the board for its concurrence. It is not within the CEO's purview to pick and choose which scheduled items to deal with or delay.

Even with the best of planning, things will change. For example, if a monitoring report is not fully accepted by the board (one section found to be noncompliant, for example), the board will want to add re-monitoring of that one "exception" to the annual work plan. This prevents any necessary follow-up work from falling through the cracks. And both the board and staff know very well the expected timelines that must be met.

Although normally every Operational Expectation and every Result policy should be scheduled for monitoring each year, it may take a year or more for the board and staff to phase in full monitoring of all such policies. The organization is being asked to do work it has never done before, and in some cases it will need time to develop new capacities to do that work well. The board and CEO jointly can decide just how much organizational stress is reasonable as early work plans are developed.

Exhibits 8.1 and 8.2 are examples of annual work plans used by organizations of various types. Some organizations meet monthly or even twice each month, while others meet quarterly or less frequently. Obviously, the fewer meetings the board has each year, the more actions each agenda must find a way to accommodate.

Questions for Thought

1. What now drives decisions about the issues that make up your board meeting agendas? Are those decisions based on any pre-designed plan of work?
2. Do you have any idea about what your board work will be at a given time during the next year?
3. How would scheduling the board's work for the next year change what it focuses on?

EXHIBIT 8.1

Nikkei Concerns Annual Work Calendar

MONTH	GC	BCR	OE	RESULTS	LINKAGE	BOARD DEVELOPMENT	OTHER BUSINESS
JAN					CAC		Shinnen Kai
FEB	3		4 (RI) 11 (M)				
MAR	6		2 (RI/M) 5 (M)		Senior Staff		Form 990 20: Board Retreat
APR	4		7 (RI) 1 (RI)				Audit 20: Reg Mtg
MAY	5		6 (RI) 4 (M)	R-2 (RI)			18: Reg Mtg
JUNE	9		9 (RI) 1 (M)	R-3 (RI)			15: Reg Mtg
JULY	10		8 (RI) 7 (M)				
AUG			3 (RI) 6 (M)				
SEPT	1		10 (RI) 9 (M)				Planning Retreat
OCT	7	1-5	11(RI) 8 (M)				CEO Sum Evaluation
NOV	2		5 (RI) 3 (M)				Budget and Nominations
DEC	8		10 (M)				

RI = reasonable interpretation M = monitoring

EXHIBIT 8.2

Sample School District Annual Work Calendar

	GC	BCR	OE	RESULTS	Board Development	Community Meetings	Other Business
REGULAR SEPT 9			3, 7				
REGULAR SEPT 23			11		Discussion of Development of Monitoring Report for OE-11, Annual Report to the Public	September 5, High School Students September 19, Middle School Parents	Governance Retreat State Assn Convention
REGULAR OCT 7			10		Update on Benchmark Testing	October 17, Employers	Wisdom Sharing Session w/Aspen Grp
REGULAR OCT 28	1, 2		12		Culturally Relevant Pedagogy, a Presentation		

(*Continued*)

EXHIBIT 8.2 *(Continued)*

	GC	BCR	OE	RESULTS	Board Development	Community Meetings	Other Business
REGULAR NOV 11	3		6		Discuss Study: Foundations for Success: Case Studies of How Urban School Systems Improve Student Achievement	November 4, Teachers/Staff	Technology & Learning Conference
REGULAR NOV 25					1. Improvement in Student Achievement, 1999–2002 2. Report on Board Community meetings	November 21, Middle School Parents	
REGULAR DEC 9		1, 2, 3, 4	14	2.1 Reading, Listening and Speaking: B/I/T		December 12, Higher Education	

REGULAR JAN 13	4	5	1	2.1 Writing: B/I/T	Parent Involvement		Complete Planning Cycle (full day) Governance Retreat & CEO evaluation (Summative)
REGULAR JAN 27			8	2.2 Math: B/I/T	Presentation of Mathematics Best Practices		
REGULAR FEB 10				2.3 Science: B/I/T	Discussion of guidance and support for students (who excel in extracurricular activities) entering college/ university	February 20, Spanish Speaking Parents	
BUDGET WK SESSION FEB 17	2, 5						

(Continued)

EXHIBIT 8.2 (*Continued*)

	GC	BCR	OE	RESULTS	Board Development	Community Meetings	Other Business
REGULAR FEB 24			9	2.4 Social Studies: B/I/T			
HOLD FOR WK SESSION MARCH 3							
REGULAR MAR 17			13	3.2, 3.3 College: B/I/T	The 2003–2004 Budget and its Impact on Board Results and Priorities		
REGULAR MAR 31			4	3.1, 3.2, 3.4 Career: B/I/T	Best Practices: Preparing Students for College and Career		Governance Retreat

OE Compliance:
RI = Reasonable Interpretation
I = Indicators
M = Monitoring Compliance Data

Results Reasonable Progress:
RI = Reasonable Interpretation
B/I/T: = Baseline, indicators/targets for achievement
M = Monitoring for Reasonable Progress

FAQs

Q: How flexible is the annual work plan?

A: By its very nature, the board's annual work plan may change at every meeting. It is intended to be a tool for scheduling the board's work. Depending on how monitoring reports are judged, engagement sessions change or are scheduled, or other work demands appear, items will be added, deleted, and moved from one meeting to another.

Q: Who maintains the calendar?

A: An administrative assistant to the board is the best choice. The person who occupies that position should be responsible for the annual work plan and its maintenance. If no such position exists, a board officer—perhaps the secretary—can do the job, but it requires serious and ongoing attention.

Q: Can the CEO change the calendar when situations arise?

A: Not without concurrence of the board.

Q: We have identified some issues in the past that needed follow-up but instead went into "a black hole," never to be heard about again. Will the work plan allow us to better control that kind of problem?

A: That is one of the primary purposes of the annual work plan: to provide a vehicle to allow the board to manage its own work, and to drive the work of staff as required to meet the board's expectations.

Chapter 9

The Board's New Meeting Agenda

Find a copy of your last board meeting agenda. Look at it closely. Now, take it outside, behind the barn. Dig a hole. Place the agenda inside. Now cover it. If you really mean what you say about your commitment to Coherent Governance®, you'll never see anything like that again!

Based on our years of experience working with boards, we have discovered something remarkable: For the most part, boards will spend their time during meetings doing almost anything the agenda asks them to do. Something else: With few exceptions, those agendas are prepared for the board by someone else, usually by the CEO.

This means that meeting after meeting, year after year, a typical board will come to meetings and spend sometimes hours and days simply responding to the recommendations offered by the CEO about matters the board may or may not agree should be the primary reasons to meet. Or, maybe even worse, these boards may be held captive to a series of extended staff reports about who knows what, whether the board has agreed that it needs to spend its time listening to such reports or not.

This does not mean that CEOs are bad people, or even that they prepare illogical or self-serving agendas—although we all know that to be the case on occasion. But what it does mean is that someone other than the board is determining what the board should do and when it should do it.

We are zealots about boards' developing and using well-constructed board meeting agendas. In fact, our conviction is that the board meeting agenda can be one of the single most important components for building an effective board. If the agenda asks the board to do the wrong work, boards usually will do the wrong work. Boards rarely reject an item placed on the agenda for them to deal with, whether it should be board work or not.

How should your agendas—and therefore your board meetings—change in a Coherent Governance® environment?

Let's review the basics. You said you wanted to:

- Move to Coherent Governance® so your board could spend time doing important leadership and governance work;
- Spend far more time on the important Results the organization is expected to achieve;
- Stop intruding into professional staff work;
- Engage both proactively and constructively with those people you serve and represent;
- Free yourself from the drudgery, the mundane "fixing things" routine you had fallen into;
- Take responsibility for your own agenda, driven by your annual work plan.

Doesn't it make sense, then, that if all these benefits are to be realized, your meetings must look dramatically different? There should be no mystery here.

The board simply needs to ask itself, "What is it that we need to spend our time doing?" What issues deserve the brainpower of five (or seven or nine, or more) board members entrusted to lead, represent and serve the owners' interest?

If the board agrees with the bulleted points above, then it must decide what should go away and what should be added to the agenda to realize these outcomes. Typically, these are the things board meetings will focus on:

- Discussing the future: Far-ranging and diverse questions to ask:
  - What will the global economy be like?
  - What kind of benefits do our customers need that we can uniquely or at least competitively provide?
  - What will our community environment be like in five years, and what kinds of skills will the workplace demand?
  - What is the gap between what students are accomplishing now and what they need to be accomplishing? What will our kids need to know to compete and succeed five years from now?
  - Are our present Results policies adequate to prepare our kids for such a future? If not, how should we change them?
- Monitoring your progress: With movement into implementation of Coherent Governance®, relatively little business meeting time should be spent monitoring performance in the GC, B/CR, and OE sections. More time

will be spent monitoring progress in the Results policy areas. Questions to ask:
  - Are the identified Results the "right" ones for our organization?
  - Are our resource allocations reasonable?
  - What are the barriers or hindrances to our progress?
  - Are there other factors or influences, internal or external, that we didn't anticipate?
  - Are subgroups of clients not being served? Why?
  - How do we engage outside resources to improve?
- Stakeholder dialogs. Questions to ask:
  - Are our Results meeting community-of-owners expectations?
  - Are the owners/members prepared to discuss data revealing levels of acceptable performance and areas of under-performance?
  - Do our owners know how we are performing?
  - With whom should we be establishing partnerships for the benefit of both our clients and our owners?
  - Are there potential resources we should be taking better advantage of?
  - Who can help speed up our progress in a given Results area?
- Resource allocation. Questions to ask:
  - Has anything changed that suggests another look at our initial resource allocation?
  - Are our plan and our priorities producing the desired results?
- Priorities. We have acknowledged that we can't do everything. Questions to ask:
  - Are our priorities achieving what we had planned for?
  - What will we not do?
  - What is the fallout from not doing it?
  - With whom should we be communicating about these priority concerns?

Do you see a pattern in these questions? They are future-oriented, not reactive in nature. They are big-picture, not "what color carpet shall we buy" issues. And they all are concerns that a governing board must consciously and responsibly address.

Of course, if you are serving on a public or government board, *some* time must be spent dealing with the mandated items imposed by the state or federal government: approve the budget, approve personnel, approve new operational policies, and other such matters.

The board can and should deal with these purely operational issues via the consent agenda, within the context of your well-defined Operational Expectations policies. Devote as little board meeting time to them as possible. Your very first OE policy requires the CEO to act legally. If state or federal law requires some specific action, the CEO cannot ignore it, whether the board makes a decision about the matter or not.

You are freed from making and remaking operational decisions because your values-based governing policies have directed and controlled operational decision-making and established rigorous accountability through scheduled monitoring.

But let's make the main point. The board decisions you make should be *policy-level* decisions, not operation-level decisions. The board's policy manual will be a dynamic document. You will have it handy at every meeting, because if you become a board that governs by policy, you will find yourself referring to a policy every time you meet, for every item on your agenda, and every time you make a decision.

And imagine this: You may have meetings of the board during which *no* decisions are made other than to adjourn. You may find yourself listening, planning, understanding, exploring options, or visioning the future without the need to decide anything. If so, you have not neglected your work. You have redefined it. You may find yourself faced with an agenda containing two or three—or maybe even only one—very focused, very deliberative discussion items.

Remember, the board is seeking depth and quality deliberation on substantive issues. You will find that you will be measuring the board's performance not on the basis of how many decisions are made during a given meeting, but on the quality of your deliberative discussion and preparation for decision-making.

SO, WHAT WILL YOUR NEW AGENDA LOOK LIKE?

We cannot decide for the board exactly what its new meeting agenda should look like, the things that should be removed, and the things that should be added. But we can offer some basic guidance based on the fundamentals of the new governing model.

Specifically, the new agenda must be built in a manner consistent with the board's job description, which is defined in policy GC-3. Why? Ask yourself this:

- Does it make sense that the board performs its job, for the most part, in the board meeting?
- And does it make sense that the board meeting agenda should be very closely aligned with the job description, virtually a mirror image?

If we can answer "yes" to these two questions, the task is half complete. We need now only to set the board's job description, GC-3, alongside the agenda and align the agenda with the policy.

Of course, it isn't quite that simple. There are some things on the board's customary agenda that it will want to keep for ceremonial or customary reasons, and others that may need to stay for legal reasons. But none of these agenda items should be centerpiece items. They should be limited in number and diminished in prominence.

The board has committed in policy to spend most of its time and attention on its Results policies. In order to do so, other kinds of items must go away or be subordinated.

Every type of organization will have some agenda components that tend to be unique to organizations of that type, but as a rule, there are some common agenda components that will serve every organization, regardless of type, very well.

- *Adopt the agenda as the first action item.* Adopting the agenda means that the board commits by majority vote that this is the board's work plan for this meeting. The reason: to keep the board focused on the issues the board itself has agreed to consider, and nothing more. The proposed agenda is not the board's agenda until the board adopts it. If any member wishes to add or remove an item (even from the consent agenda), to rearrange the order, or make any other changes to the recommended agenda, the time and means to do so is before the adoption, by the amendment process.
- *Reference each item on your agenda to an existing board policy.* If you can't find a logical fit, it may be an indicator that the topic is not board work at all! This policy reference step creates context, and prevents random discussions that tend to lower the board's focus on operations. This is work that helps the board build knowledge and understanding of its own policies, and therefore should be done by members of the board itself, not by staff.
- *Place Results discussions at the beginning of your meeting.* Staff and any audience begin to see that you mean business—customer- or client-focused business. High-performing boards spend at least 50 percent of their meetings focused on Results. Of course, if operational areas are not working as they should, or if other factors force the board's attention to them as opposed to Results, the board is doing the work it should. But if all operations are working as expected, there is no reason to dwell on such matters. The opportunity is presented to do a level of board work that most boards never find the time and occasion to do. But for you, such work now is routine!

- *Outline rules for audience or public participation*—and stick to them. This is the board's meeting, not the public's meeting. Hearing from the organization's members or from the public is proper, but they should not be allowed to dominate or redirect the board from its central purpose.
- *Identify items to be disposed of via the consent agenda.* For the most part, these are the routine matters delegated to the CEO about which the CEO is required to keep the board informed. In fact, we recommend two consent agendas. One such agenda would be a "CEO Consent Agenda" comprised of nothing more than board action on matters that have been delegated to the CEO, but are required by a state or federal law to be approved by the board. A "Board Consent Agenda" includes any matter the board chooses to place on it, any item the board does not wish to spend time discussing. These two consent agendas help keep the board and CEO issues separate, and together can save considerable board meeting time—time to spend on Results.
- *Time each section of the agenda.* Hold staff and board members to those times. Board meeting efficiency is not meant to be the primary goal, but it is important, and timed agendas can be enormously helpful.
- *Determine what staff presentations should look and sound like.* Do you want executive summaries of reports? How far in advance? Do you like PowerPoints? Would you prefer that reports not be read to you? Are all reports referenced to policy and your monitoring schedule? The board never should show up for a meeting and be held captive to a series of staff reports, all with no context, and in which the board has no interest at that time.
- *Make the final item on each agenda a verbal debriefing of the board's performance during the just-concluded meeting.* This need not be an extended conversation, nor need it be an unpleasant personalized encounter. The idea is to provide an opportunity for the board to assess what worked and what did not, so that success can be repeated and failure avoided in the future. Consider debriefing the way the military does—an "After Action Review" that strategically positions your board for continuous improvement. At the end of this chapter we offer some possible strategies for use in effective debriefing.

Sometimes the agenda may not be 100 percent "pure" or perfect according to the principles the board agreed to in Coherent Governance®. But you will see the trends: fewer items; big-picture in nature; future-oriented; and fewer decisions, with those decisions made at the policy level.

Appendix D includes actual agendas in use by boards practicing either Coherent Governance® or Policy Governance®. They generally track the provisions of the board's job description, GC-3. Use them as a starting point for the redesign of your own new agenda.

DEBRIEFING FORMATS

As with everything else in this book, there is no one accepted way to get work done. But in a broad sense, debriefing each meeting holds every board member to a higher standard of continuous improvement. Here are four ways for a board to conduct a meaningful debriefing exercise before the meeting is finally adjourned.

Option A. Three simple questions:

1. What did the board do well in our meeting?
2. What did not work well for us?
3. What do we want to do to improve?

Option B. Quick Whip Technique—around the room, and back again:

1. What elements of this meeting worked especially well?
2. What I would recommend to improve our overall performance for future meetings.

Option C. One member takes the lead:

One board member assumes the responsibility for observing the meeting and offers feedback to the board based on those observations. Other members respond to the leader's assessment with comments of their own. The role is rotated among members for each meeting.

Option D. External Monitoring Committee:

The committee is carefully chosen for balance and credibility, trained, provided with copies of appropriate policies to monitor, and sent agendas ahead of time. The committee reports back to the board with its recommendations to the board to improve its performance.

An External Monitoring Committee can be very helpful to the board, and it can be a valuable supplement to the board's self-assessment process. The following report was submitted to the board by its External Monitoring Committee, a group of stakeholders appointed by the board to observe the board's business meetings and offer constructive feedback. Members of the committee were trained in relevant policies and processes.

COMMITTEE COMPILED FEEDBACK TO THE BOARD MEMORANDUM

Date:

To: Board Vice-Chair and Liaison
External Monitoring Committee
Fr: External Monitoring Committee—First Tuesday Team
Re: Debriefing of November 6 Board Meeting

Attached below is our feedback on the November 6 School Board Meeting.
Commendation:

1. Meeting was well officiated, exuded confidence
2. Items on agenda were contextualized to relevant policy
3. Appeared that the board came prepared to the meeting
4. The CEO and CFO delivered an oral summary of OE reports and read the reasonable interpretation aloud so members could hear and consider. The board showed interest in their reports.
5. The board was very respectful of one another and of anyone presenting. There were no side conversations and there was respectful body language.
6. The board chose to be transparent in sharing its decision about the CEO and CFO compensation with the public at this forum.
7. The board chair did an excellent job of managing issues raised during the presentations.

   Example: During the presentation of the Reasonable Interpretation of OE-7 and OE-1 there were a few questions asked. The board chair noted the questions, sought clarification, asked for the questions to be held until both OE-7 and OE-1 were completed. He came back to address each issue and ensured that the person bringing up the issue was satisfied with the resolution.

To Consider:

1. Post the board agenda so that the audience understands when the board is in executive session.

   Example: The meeting officially started at 4:00 and went into executive session. The public session was started again at about 5:15 or so. It appeared to some in the audience that the board was late.

2. There appeared to be confusion about how to amend the agenda. It seems as if there should be a consistent process in place on how to amend an agenda.
3. There was no Results focus at this meeting—nothing related to student achievement
4. Display Results policies on the walls of the board room—reinforce purpose and focus of the board
5. This meeting lasted just about an hour; while none of us complained, it did make us wonder about the need for a meeting twice a month. We recognize the consent agenda was very long (about 144 pages) and realize there is a need to make sure it is approved twice a month, but we didn't really see the need for a meeting.

External Monitoring Team Needs

The External Monitoring Team wants to thank the vice-chair for sharing our needs with the appropriate members within the administration. We had what we needed to be successful for this meeting.

Questions for Thought

1. How do the sample agendas contained in appendix D compare with those used by your board?
2. What do you like about these examples? Dislike?
3. What is the relationship between the board's job description and the board meeting agenda?

FAQs

Q: Who should be responsible for developing the agendas for each board meeting?
A: The board meeting agenda is driven by the annual work plan. The board president generally meets with the CEO to develop the draft agenda. But it isn't the board's agenda until the board votes to accept it—the first action at the meeting.

Q: Who determines the policy reference for each item on the agenda?
A: Our strongest recommendation is that the board president assume that responsibility. The decision needs to be made thoughtfully, since policy references provide context for deliberation and decision-making.

Q: How do we demonstrate that our work is focused on Results, when the agenda may have pages of consent agenda items that visually clutter it and make it appear that our work is all about operations?

A: We recommend that Results focus be placed high on the agenda, and that the consent agenda and all its separate items be placed in an appendix to the agenda. The ideal is for the agenda to be shown on a single typed page, with all the detail listed elsewhere.

Q: We have groups that are accustomed to reporting to the board, which makes our meetings appear to be dog and pony shows, consuming huge amounts of board time. How do we control that issue?

A: Consider whether such reports logically fall within a Result or OE report and place them there. Also consider whether some of the reports can better be received at a work session, or presented to the CEO instead of to the board. If the board does not value such reports, they should not be a part of the meeting. The politics of this issue may require some delicate handling.

Chapter 10

Change: It's a Leadership Conundrum

Boards and organizations committed to leading and driving organizational change must overcome a number of reasonably predictable barriers in order to achieve success. It isn't easy to do. It is more difficult in some types of organizations than others.

Large public organizations, such as school districts and other governmental entities, may be some of the most challenging of all environments in which to lead change. It can be done, for sure, but boards serving such organizations must have skills and a level of determination that allow them to maintain focus and commitment in the face of resistance that organizations of other types usually never face.

We identify below some of the common barriers to sustainable organizational change and improvement. If such barriers exist, they force a board choice: Either stay the course and move forward with resolve to achieve the vision the board has for change, or allow the barriers to thwart the vision the board had when this journey started.

There is no status quo in change.

BARRIER 1: LACK OF SELF-DISCIPLINE

Admirably, boards want to honor differences of perspective and opinion among their members. But successful change efforts are marginalized by board members "playing nice" and not confronting misdirected or errant behaviors.

Lack of board discipline manifests itself in many ways: the errant chairman who chooses to exercise individual power; the board that refuses to monitor its policy on board discipline and avoids confronting a misbehaving member; the board that finds debriefing untimely and dispenses with this quality improvement necessity; the board that passively self-monitors board behavior policies because doing so rigorously might lead to confrontation.

Your board built a set of values governing board and board member behavior, and committed to monitor the board's performance against those standards. Failure to hold the board and each member accountable tells the CEO, staff, and owners that you didn't really mean it. Allowing the board or its members to misstep, or to intentionally and willfully violate its commitments, means the whole system is up for grabs. Why should any stakeholder group take the board seriously if it doesn't faithfully monitor and adhere to its own governing commitments?

Failure of the board, CEO, or staff to behave in ways that are consistent with expectations and values serves only to increase cynicism and resistance to any transformation to excellence.

You made these commitments. You thought they were important. It is essential that the board's behavior serve to honor the commitments if this transformation is to be effective and powerful.

BARRIER 2: NOT INVESTING IN BOARD DEVELOPMENT

Change for a board and organization takes time. Some change experts say sustainable change requires a minimum of five years, and that we should plan for ten.

Yet our nanosecond level of patience seduces boards into moving off course, seeking the next program of the month that they can claim credit for and use to personal advantage. Even more frequently, we witness boards that tire of the structure and drift off to the more comfortable role of making operational decisions, "managing the manager," fixing problems and engaging in discussions, and making decisions that seem to be important to "the community."

Transformation of board work and organizational focus begin with a board's sincere commitment to diagnose, address, and continuously critique its own governing style and performance. This requires a calendar that provides for continuous debriefing, time spent in conversation with one another, and retreats in order to reflect, assess, prioritize, and give clear direction.

Board development includes inside training. In Aspen, Colorado, school board veterans provide orientation for candidates for the board so they know what they are signing up for. The board provides thorough training for new board members by reviewing each policy, incorporating relevant changes, and renewing the board's mission and results. The training is conducted by the board itself, and not delegated to the administration or to associations. Members learn together, coming to understand as colleagues how the board operates as a unified body in this special environment.

Other professional development areas needed by boards become apparent as members work closely together, focused on client outcomes. The Fairfax County, Virginia, school board engaged experts to help create awareness about twenty-first-century skills. The Issaquah, Washington, school board used data experts to help build board member skills as they considered Results monitoring reports. The Columbus, Wisconsin, school board engaged experts to help board members understand how to conduct focus groups. The school board in Palm Springs, California, used the Meyers Briggs Type Indicator to help members better understand each other in order to work better together with mutual appreciation.

Although funding always is a challenge, the reality is that good governance should be worth something. A board committed to govern as well as it expects its employees to perform their jobs will recognize the need to invest reasonably in its own capacity and skill building.

BARRIER 3: NOT CREATING AN INTERNAL URGENCY FOR TRANSFORMATION

The world is changing for organizations of every type. The marketplace has new competitive realities that include pass/fail judgments.

Some wise person said that change occurs only when "the pain of change is less than the pain of remaining the same." The successful change-demanding board recognizes the growing dissent and dissatisfaction with what many consider to be the high expenditure of dollars for mediocre results.

Every organization is rife with people who assume the position "We've always done it this way; who are you to tell me to do it differently?" Why would an entrenched yet talented staff want to change the way it does business? After all, they are the professionals; they know their jobs, and they do them well. How can a part-time board possibly suggest anything different? Wounded pride, bruised egos, and professional indignation can result when the board demands change.

Audacious goals cannot be achieved by any organization when pockets of resistance work against organizational purpose, and are permitted to fester. Real board leadership must be exercised through encouragement and support for CEO efforts to take staff where they have never gone before. Strong CEO leadership will require deliberate assessment of barriers to excellent organizational performance, a compatible internal culture, and the courage to do things differently. And when some employees cannot buy into the vision for change, sometimes-tough decisions must be made by the CEO and supported by the board.

It is a battle to capture hearts and minds. And it's an important battle.

BARRIER 4: FAILURE TO COMMUNICATE

The board and its CEO must communicate strongly and frequently that *good is not good enough.* Excellent organizations create and sustain an environment that demands continuous assessment and positive, constructive support for improvement.

The old communication paradigm was to send a newsletter or a press release. Put new goals on the website. Have a community meeting. Deliver a rally call at the staff development kick-off for the new year.

Good, but not good enough. The communication from the board and CEO about their singular focus on results must be consistent and repetitive, day-to-day, hour-to-hour. Each business meeting, each speech to the Chamber of Commerce and the Lions Club, each reply to a disgruntled patron, and each and every discussion with the CEO and staff about organizational performance begins with a re-grounding in the board's focus on Results.

If the board expects change to be embraced by the owners, the board must communicate with them. The establishment of ongoing dialog about the board's Results; the changes to anticipate; honestly asking for help in diagnosing problems and barriers; encouraging questions to promote understanding before excoriating attacks are launched by the misinformed; engaging in advocacy efforts at local, state, and federal levels—all of these are issues the board needs to discuss with its owners.

The successful board of trustees reaches out and works with the people it represents, serves, and leads. That work cannot be accomplished if the board relies solely on outgoing messages and interaction with self-selected board meeting attendees.

The staff and owners must hear and see a board's long-term commitment to Results. The board must use every vehicle to communicate its vision and focus. The school boards in Issaquah, Washington, and in Aspen, Colorado, have their mission and Results prominently mounted on the walls of their boardrooms. The Fairfax, Virginia, school board has a highly interactive website easily accessible by the public, but the board also is undertaking intensive planning to work with community and parent groups around parent involvement.

Many interactive engagement strategies exist for boards to explore and use: public engagement, study circles, focus groups, electronic surveys. We strongly urge boards to consider the advisability of retaining outside professional assistance to develop a highly strategic communications plan to meet their specific board needs.

The critical keys to generating understanding and support for board and organizational efforts include asking good questions, listening well, using the feedback, and circling back for more discussion.

BARRIER 5: FAILING TO BUILD THE CORE AND REMOVE BARRIERS

The board cannot undertake this transformation in isolation. The CEO will be central to internal support and external credibility. If the CEO is a barrier, a controller, a power and prestige monger, or one who cannot accept the added accountability, the board must recognize the fact that its vision may not be achieved under those circumstances.

The CEO must lead internal organizational change. Doing so includes challenging traditional protocols, removing obstacles to change, confronting and redirecting time and people, redesigning professional development, and activating new levels of freedom and accountability. S/he is the internal organizational torchbearer.

Board members must build unity at their level, but the CEO must go shoulder-to-shoulder with the board to advance the vision. But even the board and CEO cannot perform that role in isolation.

The transformation team must include senior staff, top-level administrators, union leadership, and even community business and civic leaders who will support and advocate for the change efforts on an intimate level.

We have seen organizations where the change leader role is delegated to a staff member: the board clerk, the director of strategic planning, the chief of staff. That strategy simply does not work.

This kind of revolutionary work requires the visibility, urgency, strength, and extraordinary commitment of the senior executive with strong support from the senior administrative team. Failure to form a team characterized by such dedication means that little, if any, real change will take place. It is the *pretense of progress.*

In Columbus, Ohio, the school board and staff intimately involved the business community and union leadership. In concentrated retreat sessions and subsequent strategy committees, they built a coalition focused on strengthening the district and bolstering student achievement, all focused on the board's Results policies.

In Seattle, Washington, the Nikkei Concerns CEO has been rigorous in leading the organization's focus on accountability. He has redrafted his weekly board updates to reference each item directly to the relevant OE and Results policies. His tenacity in taking the board at its word—its policies—is serving and leading the board to greater understanding of its own governing model.

In Horry County, South Carolina, the school superintendent worked with community groups to build support for board governance and for system integrity. In addition, she and her senior staff realigned staff development and conducted twice-yearly teacher evaluations to support their efforts to increase student achievement in alignment with the board's Results policies. The team included every principal.

The lesson: Without top-to-bottom organizational alignment, support, and commitment, systemic change will not happen.

BARRIER 6: FAILURE TO KEEP IT UNDERSTANDABLE

Sometimes boards get so focused on their new governance system and its unique nomenclature they forget that there is a community of people who want to hear about the board's vision and purpose, but in plain language. Governance preoccupation and lexicon can get in the way of stakeholder acceptance and understanding. It is not the governance process you want people to focus on, but rather your vision for and necessary steps to achieve excellent organizational performance.

Some boards talk about testing their vision at the local 7-11 store. Can you say what your vision for owner and client benefits is within five minutes and without the need for a dictionary? Can you remove any language barriers that could entice people to gravitate to the negative when hearing something new and different?

Focus on the commonsense presentation of your expectations and organizational outcomes. If you can't make your work understandable to the person who does not live in your world each day, there will be no listening, no support, and eventually, no change.

BARRIER 7: FORGETTING TO ADDRESS THE LEGACY

If sustainable change is to embed itself into the fabric of the organization, the values, vision, and systems put in place by the board and its team must outlive the current players. This calls for conscious planning for the recruitment and training of new board members. It also demands great forethought and preparation for recruitment and hiring of new staff, beginning with the CEO.

If you serve on an elected governing board, it is totally reasonable to cultivate and aggressively seek out members to run for election. Find potential candidates with the demonstrated character and capacity to engage with the board and organization in a constructive manner.

The "Power of One" never ceases to amaze us. The ability of a single board member to undermine and sabotage—or to inspire and exert new levels of leadership—is unlimited. A single member can do amazing good within a group of five, seven, or nine, but a single member can be equally harmful to the effective performance of a board. Fate must not be left to chance. Effective board leadership includes building capacity for sustainability and long-term momentum.

Sustainability and legacy also are issues at the CEO level. With retirement or job change, who fills that pivotal role? Failure to recruit a CEO who understands that his or her role is to make *the board's* vision succeed can spell disaster for your change effort. Where do you recruit? Does the search firm understand your vision and how you do business? What does advertising language sound like? What kinds of critical questions must be asked during the interview?

The experience of one very sophisticated organization comes to mind, one that did not pay attention to the true character of its final candidate—beyond his pretense during the interview of understanding and supporting the board's structure. Within the first year, the board was struggling due to the CEO's complete incompatibility with the governing system. No board wants to conduct a CEO search twice in a year, so the board was faced with finding ways to compensate for the shortcoming. The board's governance focus and processes have since recovered, but not without considerable challenge and tough board direction.

BARRIER 8: IGNORING SUCCESSES

Most professions do very poor jobs of recognizing and celebrating successes. And yet we all know that encouragement increases performance.

Boards often focus excessively on what fails to work. Sometimes it pays to acknowledge what's *right*! It is all in the balance, but the scales too often are tipped toward the negative.

Boards should identify shorter-term targets that increase the likelihood that reasonable progress can be made, and then celebrate when it occurs. The journey to higher performance is hard work, and to some, alien work. Accountability is threatening. Plan for, encourage, support, and praise the short-term successes to sustain momentum. The next day with its new challenges will come with the dawn.

Our life's work is based on hoping, believing, and coaching boards and their CEOs to break down the traditional barriers and beliefs and get laser-focused on organizational performance. Doing so represents formidable change for many organizations. But we know that this country is populated by people who want to make a sustainable and constructive difference in the lives of the organizations they lead and the people those organizations serve.

Recognizing and removing barriers, externally or internally imposed, will augment the chances for successful change and attainment of that audacious vision we have for every organization's success.

Chapter 11

Now What?

Your board has made the conscious decision to transform the way it does business. Traditional board work wasn't working well. Staff-driven agendas, useless policy, individual or even party politics, endless and mind-numbing debate about minutiae and, quite probably, less-than-excellent organizational results permeated your board life.

You concluded that your board must learn to govern with excellence—doing *its* job and no one else's—in order to direct and align organizational performance to achieve Results.

Your board consciously committed to good governance and chose a state-of-the-art governing system, either Coherent Governance® or Policy Governance®, as the vehicle to get you there. At this juncture, your policies are in place, and you have implementation systems and processes ready to launch. You are confident that all systems are go, and that you are poised for a new purpose and greater rigor as a governing board. There are no storm clouds on the horizon. Life is good.

But hold on just a second. Although all the stars seem to have lined up just right at the moment, some challenging things could happen. Your board needs to anticipate and be prepared to deal with possible hazards. It is called risk management.

We encourage you to recognize that there is a least a slight chance that not everyone is as enthusiastic about your choice of a governing system as you are. These people could come from anywhere, either inside or outside the organization. They could even come from within the board itself.

The message here is that successful implementation of your new governing model is not automatically assured. In our first book, *Good Governance Is a Choice,* we discussed in chapter 11 some of the essential conditions that boards and organizations must have in order to successfully implement a new governing model. We won't repeat all those points here, but we will recap some of them, since this is such an important concern.

WHAT COULD CAUSE YOUR WORK TO FAIL?

We have seen the following conditions as contributors to failure.

Lack of commitment by the board

Common logic suggests that if the board were not committed, it would not have made the decision to adopt a new governing model in the first place. Sometimes common logic defies logic. Some boards are intrigued with the idea of doing something new and different, of being seen as trailblazing, but are less than fully committed to actually doing the work to achieve success.

Adopting a completely new and different governing model requires vigilant attention to new processes that will feel awkward for a while. Time and a little patience are necessary for the new work to gain traction.

- Resist the temptation to suspend dedicated implementation practice and do it the "old way, just this once." Commitment means consistently walking the talk about your values. Stakeholders are observing you in action to see if you meant what you said: that you would be a disciplined board, focused on the achievement of Results and not on operations.
- Resist the temptation to return to the practice of passing "resolutions" and giving informal direction to the CEO. Your commitment is to govern by policy, not by resolutions or by informal directives.
- Resist the temptation to allow staff to report on process rather than compliance or progress. This is not about being nice. It is about effective governing.
- Commit to that high standard of performance by expecting and accepting nothing less than monitoring reports that clearly and consistently give you the information and data you require to judge performance, not activity.
- Resist the temptation to tolerate poor board or board member behavior or discipline. The board is judged by the quality of its own actions. Accepting anything less than consistent compliance with the board's commitments diminishes the integrity and effectiveness of the whole board. Commitment to excellence requires honest self-reflection and courage to confront any individual or board failure.
- Resist the temptation to blame the model when the first challenge hits—as it surely will. Commitment means understanding that change is hard to

accept and is sometimes viewed with intense skepticism. Stay the course and your values for governing excellence will become clear, accepted, and welcomed.

The board's unwillingness to change old behaviors

It should be clear that adopting a different way of doing business requires old habits and customs to change. This is easy to say and always harder to do.

We are not saying that every past practice is unworthy, but rather suggesting that a board must be willing to free itself from past practice and create a culture that is based upon thoughtful exploration of what is possible, not what is comfortable. It calls for historical perspective and appreciation, but not living in history.

Failure to recognize that a new governing model will not automatically solve all old problems

Occasionally we have been invited to work with a board that is so dysfunctional that anything that floats by appears to be a life preserver. Sometimes boards find themselves in such distress that they adopt the view that if they can just adopt Coherent Governance®, all their internal problems will go away.

Typically, the problems they are dealing with are as much people problems as they are structural problems: lack of trust, poor communication, and a history of divisive behaviors.

It is true that adopting a sound operating system can provide the structure to help boards deal with the tough people problems. Governance Culture and Board/CEO Relationship policies are designed to do just that. But until the board addresses such dysfunctional conditions, no governing system in itself will make life good again for such boards.

Impatience

Changing to a new way of getting work done requires time and practice. When we work with boards, we frequently ask members to write their names on a notepad. Then we ask them to place the pen in their opposite hand, and do it again. Then we analyze what they experienced.

They typically say that the second time was slower, messier, awkward, and required more attention and thought. In general, the non-preferred hand was less efficient, with a less desirable, even childish outcome.

Implementing a new governing model can be like that. In order to become a mature board, to gain efficiency, and achieve the desired outcome, new behaviors must be learned and new skills developed. This requires time, studied practice, and patience.

Just as reading, playing golf, playing the piano, building a sports team, or becoming an excellent speaker requires time and repetition, so does the practice of good governance. This is why we strongly encourage boards to maintain an extended coaching relationship, providing an outside "eye" to identify performance issues and maintain momentum as the board transitions into the mature practice of its new governing model. Remember, even champions need coaching.

A CEO who lacks confidence in his own abilities, who is unwilling to assume accountability for independent actions, or is unsupportive of the board's new role

Some CEOs say they support the board's venture into a governing model that allows them to exercise independent leadership and to be held accountable for it. But they continue to seek board approvals for decisions that are now theirs to make—reacting out of either fear or tradition.

Some CEOs openly resist the board's new level of governing leadership and policy-level control, setting up roadblocks of infinite types. Some view this venture as a means to "control" the board, only to discover that the board actually becomes more active—but in a constructive and less intrusive way.

Other CEOs may be unwilling to change their own administrative behaviors to align the organization with the board's governing culture. They may have become very accustomed to functioning as the "leader" of the board, controlling information and giving direction to achieve their own purpose and ends.

When a board adopts Coherent Governance® or Policy Governance®, it changes not only its own way of doing business but, maybe equally dramatically, also the way the organization does its work. If a CEO either is unwilling or incapable of transforming the organization as necessary to support the board, the board's good work can be painfully slow or jeopardized.

Both Coherent Governance® and Policy Governance® can create the most freeing environments imaginable for the skilled, confident CEO. But they can be oil on water for a CEO who lacks the confidence and competence to do the job free of board approvals or who is resistant to assuming accountability for results.

Lack of support necessary for the board to succeed

Adopting a new governing model requires more support for board processes than the old system required. The board must have designated staff support to assure rigorous, accurate, and on-time monitoring records; to maintain the annual work plan; and to manage the logistics of a dialog or stakeholder engagement plan.

A board's unwillingness to deal effectively with the outliers

Even a single outlier can distract the board. Attention must be paid to those members who may not be in sync with the board majority. They come in all forms, ranging from willing but not enthusiastic, to true skeptics, to declared opponents, to outright saboteurs.

Those who are willing to join the board majority and try to make it work, despite some reservations, usually come on board. Their views are important and must be heard. Over time, there is a good chance that the board's success will elevate their level of support.

It is the opponents and the saboteurs who concern us. These are the members who not only oppose what the majority is doing, but also try to assure that the whole venture fails. Their overt and covert behaviors can take several forms, but you know them by their actions.

A board cannot allow individual members to divert its attention or waste its time. Nor can it allow the destructive behavior of a single member, or a distinct minority, to determine the board's fate. We still govern in a democracy, by majority rule. A number of possible remedies are available to the board to help deal with destructive behaviors, and they must be used as the board continues to seek to build unity and focus.

Failure to recognize that the model is a means, not the end

Adopting a new governance operating system is an important step for any board. At the beginning, there are new processes and behaviors to learn. It takes careful attention by the members to learn how to use the new tools available to the board.

But we have seen boards become so consumed with "getting it right" that they became slaves to the system—the mechanics of doing the work—rather than focusing on the outcomes the system was designed to produce. They focus on the process with rigorous devotion rather than using the model as a way to get board work done.

There is a high level of discipline required for a board to live with the commitments it has made in policy. Nevertheless, within a reasonable period of time, the board and staff should be comfortable with this operating system as their adopted platform and practice, using it to focus on achieving Results.

WHAT TO DO WHEN PROBLEMS HIT

Sooner or later, your governing model will become a target. Count on it. It will happen. The only things we don't know are where the challenge will come from, and when it will happen.

If you are a public board, such as a public school board, it likely will happen fairly soon. The environment in which you work is volatile and visible, as well as laden with a full range of emotions and differing opinions about every decision. That environment presents easy opportunities for people to challenge everything—your governing model included. Even if how you make decisions and how the organization is governed have nothing whatsoever to do with the matters that concern people, they likely will label your governing model as the cause of whatever the real issue is.

Once the organization experiences a problem or makes a decision with which some people disagree, the board should be prepared to deal with charges that it has "given away the store" to the CEO. The board has "abdicated its responsibilities," and no longer is in charge. "Why even have a board," people will ask, "if it refuses to make decisions?" (All about operational issues, of course.)

Such challenges and criticism could come from within the organization, from staff or their organizations. Or criticism may come from outside the organization, from organized groups or influential individuals. The more inflammatory the issue, the stronger the challenge to the governing model will be. The board will be tempted by these groups to "get itself back in charge" and "do its duty" by overturning the decision that caused such uproar.

Occasionally, the problems may be real. For example, the CEO may make a decision that runs counter to the board's values, and the board is required to respond in some fashion. In the old way of doing business, the board likely would jump into the middle of the issue and "fix it."

But whether the criticism is based on a real problem or not, it still becomes a challenge to the board's governing system. And it presents to the board an opportunity to respond. How would a board response in this new governing environment be any different from the way it might have responded under its old way of doing business?

A board's best course of action in any such challenge is to use the tools its governing model provides. We frequently say to boards as they are first launching their practice of the model that what they have is a shiny new toolbox, just loaded with all kinds of neat tools. Simply owning the tools is of little value to the board, however. In order to gain any real benefit, the board must actually use the tools as they were intended to be used.

These tools—your policies and the proper use of the processes we discuss in this book—are the board's best means for dealing with challenges such as those mentioned above. People who fail to understand the power of this system that delegates decision-making—but holds the people who make decisions accountable—need educating. And the board should be skilled in using the tools to demonstrate accountability, whether decisions are controversial or not.

Effectively monitoring organizational performance is an ongoing role of the board. If stakeholders both inside and outside the organization see the board doing its job on an ongoing basis, they will be less likely to challenge the system when a decision is made that they don't like.

The board has opportunity to monitor any policy at any time there is need to do so. When criticisms are leveled, sometimes the board's logical course of action may be to monitor the relevant policy, and let the resulting decision about whether conditions are compliant answer the criticism. The judgment of the board should be not whether any staff action was the "right" action or not, but whether the action was based on a reasonable interpretation of and is compliant with the board's policy. This prevents the board from second-guessing staff decisions. It also demonstrates the board's role in assuring both reasonable staff performance and acceptable board oversight.

What the board must avoid is yielding to the temptation to "suspend the model just this one time to deal with this extraordinary problem." There is no organizational condition or problem that Coherent Governance® or Policy Governance® cannot provide the means for the board to effectively deal with—that is, if the board understands how to use the tools in its toolbox!

POTHOLES, NOT ROADBLOCKS

Let us make one point very clear: we have written in these last two chapters about conditions that *could*, if left unaddressed, jeopardize a board's own governing success and its efforts to forge organizational change and transformation. It is our fervent hope that your board will avoid the need to deal with any of them. But if they do rear their ugly heads, recognize them for what they are: they are *potholes*; they are not *roadblocks*.

Repeatedly, we have seen dedicated boards and board members confront and deal effectively with every one of these barriers and challenges in ways that are nothing short of heroic. We know the lost momentum the board experiences when its focus is diverted to deal with them, but that sometimes is the nature of change. It doesn't come easily, but the result is worth the effort.

Your board and your organization have taken some significant steps toward creating a bold and exciting future. You will hit some bumps along the way. Don't let them deter your vision and diminish your commitment to build something bigger and better. Nurture what you have given birth to. It will grow into something that will make you proud.

Appendix A

Monitoring Operational Expectations Policies for Compliance

Author's note: At the point of this book's publication, this school board and district are only a few months into implementation of Coherent Governance®. They are "textbook clean" in their interpretations and selection of indicators of compliance. The CEO and staff are setting themselves, the board, and district up for great success when the evidence is later presented.

Harrison School District 2

Operational Expectations Monitoring Document—OE-9

Disposition of the Board:
Date:
Re-monitoring Date:

________________ In Compliance

________________ Not in Compliance

________________ Compliance with Noted Exceptions

Summary statement/motion of the board: ________________________

____

____

____

Certification of the Superintendent: I certify this report to be accurate.

Signed: ______________________________, Superintendent

Date: ______________________________

OE-9: Communicating with the Public	CEO		BoE	
The superintendent shall assure that the public is adequately informed about the condition and direction of the district.	In Compliance	Not in Compliance	In Compliance	Not in Compliance
SUPERINTENDENT Interpretation: • The superintendent interprets the public to mean the district's parents and community stakeholders. • The superintendent interprets adequately informed to mean that the public receives communications from the district in a variety of ways about the district. • The superintendent interprets messages about the district's condition to include information about the organization's finances, academic results, climate or honors (awards and recognition). • The superintendent interprets messages about the district's direction to include communication about the district's action plan, programs, changes, innovations or initiatives.				

Superintendent Indicators of Compliance: • In a random survey sample of district residents, administered before 1 July 2011, at least 75 percent of the respondents will express they were "adequately informed" about the condition and direction of the District.				
Board Comments:				
OE-9.1				
1. Assure the timely flow of information, appropriate input, and strategic two-way dialog between the district and the citizens that builds understanding of the district's condition and direction.				
SUPERINTENDENT Interpretation: • The district interprets timely flow to mean that we, at least quarterly, communicate to the public through a variety of mediums throughout the year. • The district interprets appropriate input to mean that a useful and accommodating means for hearing the thoughts, concerns, questions, and ideas of our staff, parents, and community members is in place. We are clear about how stakeholders can give input/feedback and how it can be most useful.				

• The district interprets strategic two-way dialog to mean that we engage the public, at least quarterly, in conversations around the district's condition and direction to build understanding and relationships. • The district interprets builds understanding and support to mean that our communication efforts help stakeholders become informed about the district's direction and progress, and hold a positive perception of the district.				
SUPERINTENDENT Indicators of Compliance: • In a random survey sample of district residents, administered before 1 July 2011, at least 75 percent of the respondents will express they were "adequately informed" about the condition and direction of the District and show support for district initiatives.				
Board Comments:				
OE-9.2				
2. Prepare and publish, on behalf of the board, an annual progress report to the public that includes the following items: a. Data indicating student progress toward accomplishing the board's Results policies. b. Information about school district strategies, programs and operations intended to accomplish the board's Results policies.				

c. Revenues, expenditures and costs of major programs and a review of the district's financial condition.				
SUPERINTENDENT Interpretation: • The district interprets publish to mean that it will make the "annual progress report to the public" available via print and online.				
Board Comments:				

Author's note: San Diego Unified School District CEO and staff diligently worked to provide spot-on interpretations, a choice of authentic indicators, and then clear compliance data against those indicators. We think they have done an excellent job. This report is abbreviated.

SAN DIEGO UNIFIED SCHOOL DISTRICT

Operational Expectations Monitoring Report

OPERATIONAL EXPECTATION—11: Communicating with the Board

Date:

Disposition of the Board:	Date for Re-monitoring: July

	Compliance
	Not in Compliance
X	Compliance with Noted Exception

Summary Statement/Motion of the Board:	

Chair: ________________ Superintendent: ________________

OE–11: Communicating with the Board	Supt		Board	
The superintendent shall assure that the board is fully and adequately informed about matters relating to board work and significant organizational concern.	In Compliance	Not in Compliance	In Compliance	Not in Compliance
		X		

Superintendent's Board-Approved Interpretation

The board values having a breadth of facts, knowledge, information and trend analysis provided to it by the superintendent on issues relating to its job of governing the district as delineated in its Results policies, Board/Superintendent Relations, Governance Culture, and Operational Expectations.

Superintendent's Board-Approved Indicator:

We will know we are compliant when:

The board is regularly provided with thorough information through the various communication tools, including, but not limited to, formal monitoring reports as scheduled, the mailing of the board's Friday Packets, emails, memos and reports from staff, the finance division's regular financial reports and budget updates.

Superintendent's Evidence of Compliance

1. The board receives from the superintendent and cabinet members weekly Friday Packets, which include updates on ongoing work. The board also regularly receives memos and emails on a variety of issues arising at sites or for the district as a whole. When the matter is of such a significant, sensitive, or emergency nature, the superintendent personally calls each board member to inform and discuss the issue(s).
2. In accordance with the board's Annual Work plan calendar, the board approved the Monitoring Report for Operational Expectation 10 (OE-10), Asset Protection, on April 27 as compliant. The board

approved Operational Expectation 9 (OE-9), Facilities Monitoring Report, on May 25 as compliant with exceptions. Operational Expectation 6 (OE-6), Financial Planning, was scheduled for monitoring by the board on June 22. Given the extraordinary pressures imposed on the district by the state and changing financial impacts to the district, staff was unable to devote the time needed to develop the monitoring data for OE-6 Financial Planning in June, but has submitted the monitoring **report to the board** for July 27. Operational Expectation (OE-5) Personnel Administration was scheduled for Monitoring on July 13. Staff has now submitted the OE-5 monitoring report for board review on July 27.

3. The superintendent's direction to the cabinet has been, and will continue to be, that staff needs to adhere to the board's Annual Work Plan Calendar. All Operational Expectations should be monitored in this calendar year and the board's Goals for Student Achievement Work Group progress will be reported on each month at a regularly scheduled board meeting. An initial set of indicators for the Goals for Student Achievement will be submitted for board consideration and action in the first semester of this calendar year.
4. In order to provide the board with a regular reporting on financial matters, beginning in September, Finance will provide to the board a monthly overview of the status of the budget and overall fiscal health of the district.

While we believe we are not fully compliant at this particular point in time, we believe we are substantially compliant with the board's policy statement. It is expected that during this school year, we will become fully compliant with this Board Policy Statement and the board approved indicator.

Board Comments:

Author's note: This is a sample OE monitoring report from a self-insurance pool. It is technically consistent with our implementation counsel, but we would recommend that the interpretations be combined with their choice of indicators. The report will improve as the evidence of compliance is shown separately from process, which should be reported under a separate heading. The report is abbreviated, but it provides a snapshot of good work being done in this organization, now known as Enduris Washington. The interpretations are clear and the evidence reasonably thorough.

OPERATIONAL EXPECTATIONS 4: PERSONNEL ADMINISTRATION

I certify that the information in this report is true.

Signed: ______________________ Date: ______________________

Mark A. Kammers, CEO

Disposition of the Board

______________________ Compliance

______________________ Not in compliance

Signed: ______________________ Date: ______________________

Vicki Carter, Chair

OE 4: Personnel Administration	**CEO**		**Board**	
	Compliance	Not in compliance	Compliance	Not in compliance
The CEO shall assure the recruitment, employment, development, evaluation and compensation of employees in a manner necessary to enable the pool to achieve its *Results* policies and that is consistent with the *Operational Expectations* of the board.	X			

CEO Interpretation:

I interpret this policy to mean that the CEO will hire and retain skilled, professional, highly qualified, and competent employees that are continually trained to assure they are knowledgeable and understand all policies, and are committed to achieving the End Results and Operational Expectations of the board.

CEO Indicators and Evidence of Compliance

WGEP has Administrative Policy 302: Hiring Procedures that requires a job description for every position, addresses the recruitment of highly qualified persons, adopts associated salary ranges and benefits packages designed to meet the needs of the organization, and follows board policy. Every position at WGEP has a complete job description that outlines the job responsibilities and the minimum requirements of job candidates. WGEP participates in salary and benefits surveys to inform on the compensation necessary to attract the highly qualified candidate.

Annual performance evaluations include a discussion about personal and career development planning that results in a training plan for the next year. A training budget allows for staff to advance their skills through various forms of training. In addition, administrative staff is required to attend customer service training on an annual basis. Management staff is required to attend AGRiP Leadership conferences on an annual basis.

To ensure that staff is competently performing their duties, the director of administration and human resources is assigned to supervise the day-to-day operations of the organization.

Employee performance is evaluated on an annual basis and is based on recognizing excellence in performance. The employee's contribution to meeting the End Results and Operational Expectations, and establishing targets for personal improvement will be added to their next performance evaluation.

4.1 The CEO will conduct extensive background inquiries and checks prior to hiring any paid personnel.	X		

CEO Interpretation

I interpret this policy to direct the CEO to ensure that every new employee undergo a thorough background investigation as permitted by law as part of the hiring process.

CEO Indicators and Evidence of Compliance

WGEP has Administrative Policy 302: Hiring Procedures to conduct pre-employment background investigations. The investigation abides by state and federal law regarding the rights of potential employees under the Fair Credit Reporting Act and the use of criminal histories. A complete background investigation includes past employment, references, criminal conviction history, credit check if appropriate, and traffic violation/accident history.

WGEP hired one new employee in policy year 2007. The employee underwent a thorough background investigation.

Author's note: The sample report below is from a school district and is a report on the board's OE-2: Emergency CEO Succession. The CEO took advantage of the opportunity to educate the board in this well-done report.

__________ School District

Operational Expectations Monitoring Report

I certify that the information in this report is true.

Signed: ________________________ Date: ________________________

Superintendent

Disposition of the Board Date for Re-monitoring: ________________

__________ Compliance

__________ Not in Compliance

__________ Compliance with Exception

Signed: ________________________ Date: ________________________

Board President

Comments: ____

____

____

____

OE-2 Emergency CEO Succession	CEO	CEO	BoE	BoE
The CEO shall designate at least one other executive staff member who is familiar with the board's governance process and issues of current concern and is capable of assuming CEO responsibility on an emergency plan.	In Compliance	Not in Compliance	In Compliance	Not in Compliance
	XXX			

Interpretation

I interpret this policy to require the preparation of current personnel to manage essential functions and urgent matters on a temporary basis—as distinct from preparation for the job as a whole. This interpretation excludes long-term planning, decision-making about the organizational structure, informal conventions and expectations of the superintendent's office currently in effect, and the superintendent's professional roles outside the district. Further, my interpretation does not presume present, detailed knowledge of all essential functions, but awareness of primary needs, knowledge of resources for the management of each, and the ability to access those resources in an appropriate and timely manner.

Evidence of Compliance

The current organizational structure has a deputy superintendent and three assistant superintendents: assistant superintendent for business services, human resources, and administrative services.

I affirm that the deputy superintendent and assistant superintendents are sufficiently familiar with board and superintendent issues and processes and could take over with reasonable proficiency as an interim successor. The primary emergency plan in the absence of the CEO is for the deputy superintendent to assume responsibilities. In the deputy superintendent's absence, the assistant superintendent of human resources, assistant superintendent of business services, assistant superintendent of administrative services would be in charge, in that order.

1. The deputy and assistant superintendents work directly with and contribute to the following essential functions of the superintendent:
   - Regular support in cabinet meetings, including the preparation of materials for board meetings
   - Monitoring of and fulfilling requirements of board's mission, goals, OEs and Results policies.
   - Implementation of district governance work plan
   - Overall management of board level goals, communications, problem-solving, evaluation procedures, and inter-relatedness of cabinet and all administrative meetings.
2. The deputy and assistant superintendents have access to the policies, procedures, legal services and other human resources necessary to
   - conduct investigations and resolve formal complaints
   - make decisions associated with litigation
   - respond to compliance requirements
   - manage the budget process
   - manage meetings in accordance with the Brown Act
3. Through weekly administrative cabinet and bi-monthly board meetings, the deputy and assistant superintendents are routinely in touch with the major issues and work in progress of the superintendent and board.
4. Knowledge of other essential matters and commitments is retrievable from the administrative team, support staff, and common calendars.

Author's note: The Racine Unified School District staff has done excellent work in producing increasingly good reports. Their interpretations and compliance data are clear and comprehensive. The next step in this evolutionary process is to separate out the indicators of compliance, and to strengthen the evidence of compliance. This report is edited for brevity.

Racine Unified School District
OE-10 Instructional Program Monitoring Report

SUPERINTENDENT CERTIFICATION

With respect to Operational Expectation 10 (Instructional Program), taken as a whole, the superintendent certifies that the proceeding information is accurate and complete, and is:

__________ In Compliance

____X____ In Compliance, with Exceptions (as noted in the evidence)

__________ Not in Compliance

Signed: ____________________ Date: ____________________
Superintendent

BOARD OF EDUCATION ACTION

With respect to Operational Expectation 10 (Instructional Program), the board:

__________ Accepts the report as fully compliant

__________ Accepts the report as compliant with noted exceptions

__________ Finds the report to be noncompliant

Summary statement/motion of the board:

____

____

____

Signed: ____________________ Date: ____________________

Board President

Racine Unified School District

Operational Expectations Monitoring Report

OE:10 Instructional Program

The superintendent shall maintain a program of instruction that offers challenging and relevant opportunities for all students to achieve at levels defined in the board's *Results* policies.

The superintendent will:

Interpretation

The board values that the program used to teach students is demanding and stimulating, designed to push students to higher levels of achievement in pursuit specifically of the board's stated values for student achievement in the Results policies.

The board values an instructional program that is designed based on the best practices in the areas of curriculum, instruction, assessment and social interaction. Our interpretation for each of these components is below. The Teaching and Learning Framework provides a structure for organizing these big ideas around student learning. We interpret:

- Curriculum is the knowledge, content, and skills that are written, taught, and assessed. The curriculum is based off of state standards that are broken down into learning targets at each grade and subject level. Enduring understandings or big rocks are identified as essential ideas to be learned. Essential or guiding questions help to focus student learning on the enduring understandings.
- Instruction is the methodology used to convey the curriculum.
- Assessment has two major components: formative and summative. The purpose of formative assessment is to check for students' understanding and adjust instruction accordingly. Summative assessment is designed to formally assess what students know and are able to do.
- Social interaction recognizes that all learning is constructed through experiences and interaction with peers, teachers, and the environment.

10.1 Ensure that instructional programs are based on a comprehensive and objective review of best practices research.	*Compliant*

Interpretation

The board values an instructional program that is developed with full awareness of the work and practices of current research, other districts' practice and educators. Further, it values that the study of other works to be done without bias—allowing for full review and openness to bring those practices to our district.

Evidence of Compliance

According to the National Research Council's publication, *How People Learn* (copyright 2000), and additional research by Zemel, Daniels, and Hyde's *Best Practice: Today's Standards for Teaching and Learning in America's Schools* (copyright 2005), best practices in education can be divided into four major categories.

1. Student-centered: Students learn best when the material is relevant to their lives. Learning activities must be challenging, yet attainable. Hands-on and active learning are the most powerful forms of learning.
2. Cognitive: Activities that focus on higher-order thinking skills for all students are essential. Students must create or re-create meaning using all modes of learning.
3. Social: Learning is experience-based. Students must be given opportunities to interact with one another and their teachers in a manner that creates opportunities for success.
4. Knowledge-based: Experts organize problems differently from novice learners. Deep understanding of content-based issues is a hallmark of a knowledge-based learner.

As part of the district effort to bring coherence to a vision for teaching and learning a framework was adopted that incorporates the elements described above. This framework incorporates work by Grant Wiggins and Jay McTighe's *Understanding by Design* and the Instructional Process initiative into Racine's Teaching and Learning Framework. This North Star Framework for Teaching and Learning is depicted on the following page [*author's note: framework not included here for brevity*].

As new research is published, current practices are evaluated and amended. Continuous Progress, used for the elementary reading, has been modified to retain the essential tenet that students are taught at the appropriate instructional level, while exposing students to grade-level knowledge, concepts and skills through differentiated instruction.

As the curriculum section of the instructional management system, SchoolNet, is developed this summer, a comprehensive repository for the instructional program will be accessible to all staff and parents. The framework will be included in the SchoolNet software as a way to structure curriculum, assessment and instruction. Professional development to deepen understanding of this model is in the planning stages and will be introduced at the Shared Leadership Academy. This work will begin this summer and be updated on a yearly basis.

10.2 Base instruction on academic standards that meet or exceed state and/or nationally recognized model standards.	*Compliant*

Interpretation

We interpret "base instruction . . ." to mean the district's core instructional program that all students receive.

We interpret ". . . meet or exceed state and/or nationally recognized model standards" to mean that the district's instructional program is based on the Wisconsin State Model Academic Standards.

The board values district curriculum and instructional programs designed to meet levels approved by the federal government—assuring our program is competitive with other districts throughout the states. As a result, the Board of Education adopted state standards as the district's local standards, as well. Curriculum guides are written to correlate with the Wisconsin State Model Academic Standards.

Evidence of Compliance

The Wisconsin Model Academic Standards are the basis for district curriculum writing projects. The state standards are based on national standards developed by national and international organizations (i.e., International Reading Association, National Council for Teachers of Math, etc.).

Research that is supported by these various organizations and others is the foundation for the Wisconsin Model Academic Standards. Currently, the district is breaking down the state standards by grade and subject area to provide teachers with clear subject and grade level targets. This work is completed in the following grade levels and subject areas:

- Mathematics, grades K–8
- English Language Arts, grades K–8
- Social Studies, grades K–12
- Physical Education, grades K–12
- Career and Technology Education

This summer, the following subject areas and grade levels will be complete:

- Science, grades K–12
- Mathematics, grades 9–12
- English, grades 9–12

As stated in 10.1, this work will be available to staff and parents via SchoolNet. Professional development will be structured around this framework and its components, as well.

10.3 Align curriculum with the standards.	*Compliant*

Interpretation

The board values that what we teach students is directly related to the achievement of the adopted state and local standards.

We interpret "align curriculum" to mean that instruction is based on the Wisconsin State Model Academic Standards and that the content, knowledge, skills, assessments and the selection of materials are based on these standards.

Evidence of Compliance

During the summer, Curriculum and Instruction coordinators and supervisors [with teams of teachers] develop curriculum guides. Curriculum guides link units of instruction to the Wisconsin Standards.

Capacity Building

These guides exist for all core academic areas and many elective areas. Summer curriculum writing will include rewrites and updates for the following courses:

- English 11
- CP Geometry
- Health 9
- Elementary Physical Education
- US History
- AP World History
- Science, grades 6–8
- Science, grade 9

10.4 Effectively measure each student's progress toward achieving or exceeding the standards.	*Compliant*

Interpretation

The board values that all students' work is evaluated with reliability and validity against their progress toward or surpassing identified standards.

We interpret “effectively measure” to mean that the district uses formative and summative assessment tools to determine students’ progress in achieving the North Star vision. More specifically, the summative assessment tools include the Wisconsin Knowledge and Concepts Exams (WKCE). The formative assessment tools include the Northwestern Evaluation Association’s Measures of Academic Progress (NWEA MAP).

Evidence of Compliance

The district measures student process against the state standards in core academic areas using the Wisconsin Knowledge and Concepts Exams (WKCE), which are aligned to the Wisconsin State Standards. Several core academic content areas have begun to create common formative and summative assessment measures to further increase knowledge regarding student progress. Additionally, the district also measures student progress in reading and mathematics three times a year in grades 2–9 using the Measures of Academic Progress.

Capacity Building

Although we can effectively measure student progress and have processes in place to do so, staff access to these data can be cumbersome and difficult. The Instructional Management System, SchoolNet, will house the assessments mentioned above. This will provide staff and our parents/guardians easy access to student achievement data that can be used to drive instruction.

These data will be loaded prior to the August 9 Shared Leadership Data Retreat.

Appendix B

Monitoring Results for Reasonable Progress

Author's note: This first report is from Nikkei Concerns, an organization that provides support and healthcare for elders in the Seattle area. The new executive director is doing a good job in taking the first steps in laying out the reasonable interpretation for the board. If you were on the board, would you believe the new CEO understands your value? The indicators are ambitious. And the CEO has taken the opportunity to inform the board of his plans to meet this Result in Capacity Building. Shortly, he will provide baseline data and establish targets.

NIKKEI CONCERNS MISSION
POLICY TYPE: RESULTS

Our mission is to enrich and support the lives of elders and meet their needs in a way that honors and respects the Nikkei culture and values.

R-2: As a result of our efforts, our elderly will maintain the highest possible quality of life, including physical and mental health and wellness.

REASONABLE INTERPRETATION

I interpret this policy to mean that the board values our elders, as they age:

- *Elders*—Defined as all individuals who can benefit from current and future services of Nikkei Concerns.

- *The highest quality of life*: Enjoy a lifestyle, to the extent possible, that our elders are accustomed to that supports personal goals, choice, dignity, and respect in a safe, enriching, and homelike environment. They will have meaningful and consistent relationships with family, friends, social groups, and community; enjoy and practice their cultural traditions, language, food, values, and spirituality; engage in a diversity of activities and areas of interest; and continue to have access to and a place in the broader community and world.
- *Physical health and wellness*: Enjoy, to the extent possible, their fullest potential of mobility and appearance while mitigating any pain and illness to support their independence, self-worth, and quality of life.
- *Mental health and wellness:* Enjoy, to the extent possible, their emotional and cognitive well-being and exercise their intellect and interests while mitigating any behavioral illnesses to support their independence, self-worth and quality of life.

Quality of life, physical and mental health, and wellness extends to areas including self-determination, social, family, spiritual, cultural, and environment.

INDICATORS/EVIDENCE OF COMPLIANCE

- Utilizing current and future clinical systems and mechanisms (Quality Assurance Meetings), measures (e.g., MDS, QIS/State Surveys, Quality Indicators/ADLs, etc.) and experts to create a platform to continuously evaluate and upgrade services.
- 75 percent of our elderly will respond to Nikkei Concerns' "Customer Satisfaction Surveys" that they feel they are able to maintain their highest possible quality of life, including physical and mental health and wellness via or in part by Nikkei Concerns' programs and services.
- 75 percent of our elderly family members will respond to Nikkei Concerns' "Customer Satisfaction Survey" that their loved one is able to maintain the highest possible quality of life, including physical and mental health and wellness via or in part by Nikkei Concerns' programs and services.

PROCESS/CAPACITY BUILDING

We will accomplish this through our efforts of:

- Committing to a resident and participant centered and directed approach.

- Creating goals, objectives, standards of operations, systems and measures reflective of a "premier" organization that honors and respects our elderly.
- Proactively enhancing and expanding current programs and services through identification of "best practices" and trends. Ongoing educational efforts to entire Nikkei community including health care conferences, online resources, and one-to-one consultations.
- Ensuring we engage high quality staff and business partners (vendors) and actively involve volunteers and family members in support of our elderly by providing appropriate resources and trainings.
- Maintaining compliance to all laws and regulations including "Resident's Rights."
- Creating a strategic plan that supports meeting the needs of our evolving elderly community.
- Developing and implementing an overall budget and allocating appropriate resources to support the organizational and our elderly goals, objectives and culture

Author's note: This second sample is from Eden Prairie, Minnesota. The staff is making good progress in presenting clear, digestible reports for board consideration of reasonable progress. Trend line charts were not included here, for brevity.

Eden Prairie Schools

Academic Achievement Monitoring Report

Results Policy R-2—Science

Criteria for Board Review: Results Policies

1. The policy has been reasonably interpreted.
2. The organization is making reasonable progress toward achieving the board's stated results.
3. The information is sufficient to allow the board to decide.
4. The board will be looking for performance over time, trend lines moving in the right direction, steps that are being taken to improve, and reasons why improvement is or is not occurring.

Certification of the CEO: *I certify this report to be accurate.*

We assert that the organization is not making reasonable progress toward achieving the board's stated results in science.

Date:

__________________________CEO

Summary statement of the board: Motion made by Ross, seconded by Mueller, to accept the report as asserted by administration as not making progress and as amended to treat criteria #4, steps being taken to improve, as an exception to the report with that section to be re-monitored in March and to have the high school improve participation rates for science to be on par with the participation of other subjects that have high stakes testing and to review the nature of indicators to determine if there is a better way to report results.

Result: Academic Achievement Science R-2
All students will stretch to achieve academic excellence without racial predictability and graduate prepared for post-secondary options.

2.2 All students will apply the knowledge or skills acquired from the following academic disciplines to ensure a broad range of post-secondary opportunities and career choices:

- Reading
- Writing
- Math
- Science
- Social studies

Interpretation of Result R-2.2 for Science

Our understanding of the board values as related to this policy are as follows:

The district has interpreted "achieve academic excellence" to mean science proficiency for all students using Minnesota science academic standards and state MCA-II and MTAS science assessments. Every child, according to their ability, will have the science knowledge and skills required for a variety of opportunities in post-secondary and career options.

We have determined that students who "graduate prepared for post-secondary options" in science should be proficient in scientific methodology. Students will be able to objectively investigate the natural world, interpret data, and apply their knowledge and problem-solving skills to the science-related setting.

We have interpreted "students will apply the knowledge and skills" to mean that students will be proficient in the major elements found in the scientific process (able to form solid hypothesis, isolate variables, conduct observations noticing relationships and patterns, collect evidence, aggregate and analyze qualitative and quantitative data, graphically or statistically represent data, analyze error, and support or refute the hypothesis). In high school level science lab opportunities students are able to demonstrate their knowledge and skills against a common rubric measuring the critical components of experimental design.

We have interpreted "stretch" to mean that students personally conduct a variety of inquiry-based experiences to apply their knowledge and problem-solving skills.

Students also have the opportunity to "stretch" by completing advanced (enriched, advanced, and AP) science courses.

The district uses Minnesota state science standards and the MCA-II Science and MTAS Test to measure progress in science knowledge and skills at grades 5 and 8, and after a student has taken biology (students typically take biology in tenth grade).

Terms

Capacity Building—Additional steps needed to make reasonable progress.

Common Assessments—Local assessments developed during the Curriculum Improvement Cycle (CIC) and aligned to meet local and state academic standards.

MCA II—The Minnesota Comprehensive Assessments—Series II are the state tests that meet the requirements of No Child Left Behind (NCLB). To date the MCA-II Science test does not include measures of adequate yearly progress (AYP) under NCLB. New MCA III Science standards were released in June. Students will be assessed on these new standards in spring two years from now.

MTAS—Minnesota Test of Academic Skills—Alternative reading, math, and science assessments to MCA II designed for students with the most significant cognitive disabilities.

Science Standards—Standards were developed by the Minnesota Department of Education (MDE) for Science. A copy of these standards is available upon request or can be found on the MDE website. These standards are assessed by MCA II assessments in grades 5, 8, and after students take high school biology (typically tenth grade at EPHS).

Subgroups—Groups of students identified by the Minnesota Department of Education and NCLB based on: race/ethnicity; EL (English Learners); SPED (students receiving special education services); and FRP (students receiving free or reduced priced lunch).

Trend data—This monitoring report focuses performance over time. Science MCAs were first administered in the 2007–2008 school year. Research shows that when looking at trend data it is important to look at data covering a three- or four-year span. When we look at our trend data internally, we consider both growth and regression to be significant with results that exceed 5 percentage points. Significant growth is reflected by "+"; significant regression is reflected by "-"; and "=" is used when growth or regression is less than 5 percentage points.

Executive Summary

We assert that the organization is not making reasonable progress toward achieving the board's stated results in science.

- This report provides four achievement indicators (three on MCA results and one on Common Assessments at the high school) and three stretch indicators.
- Our interpretation of not making reasonable progress rests on the lack of significant growth in science achievement at grades 5, 8, and the high school.
- We observe an overall drop in stretch course participation rates at Central Middle School and a drop in some subgroups at the High School.
- In grade 5, four of ten cells reflect achievement regression in MCA results, while the remaining six cells lack significant change in achievement. Additionally all cells are significantly below target.
- In grade 8, eight of ten cells show improvement in achievement levels on the Science MCA with white, Asian, and special education students making the greatest gains. Overall, however, achievement levels are not reflective of reasonable progress.
- At the high school some subgroups are seeing gains on the MCA. Much of the data seems to indicate stagnant growth and all subgroups are performing below expected growth rates. The Common Assessment data is more positive but significant achievement gaps still exist, especially with our black, Hispanic, EL, and FRP students. We observe that two different assessment tools present us with two different achievement profiles.

Indicator 1 **MCA Science** **Grade 5**	**Subgroups**	**Trend**			**Targets**		**3-yr Trend**	**n 2010**
All students will demonstrate proficiency on the MCA-II and MTAS Science test in fifth grade. ** Less than ten students were in this subgroup		MCA/ MTAS 2008	MCA/ MTAS 2009	MCA/ MTAS 2010	Target 2010	Target 2011	+ / –	n
	All	50%	54%	48%	60%	58%	=	692
	White	53%	58%	54%	64%	64%	=	520
	Black	29%	23%	24%	27%	34%	–	82
	Hispanic	35%	29%	21%	31%	31%	–	24
	Asian	47%	56%	42%	62%	52%	–	64
	Am. Indian	**	**	**	**	**	**	2
	SPED	31%	43%	32%	39%	42%	=	91
	EL	3%	0%	0%	10%	10%	=	25
	FRP	22%	27%	24%	30%	34%	=	135
	Female	50%	43%	44%	**	54%	–	321
	Male	49%	64%	52%	**	62%	=	371

Indicator 2 MCA Science Grade 8	**Subgroups**	**Trend**			**Targets**		**3-yr Trend**	**n 2010**
All students will demonstrate proficiency on the MCA-II and MTAS Science test in eighth grade. ** Less than ten students were in this subgroup		MCA/ MTAS 2008	MCA/ MTAS 2009	MCA/ MTAS 2010	Targets 2010	Targets 2011	+ / –	n
	All	49%	58%	63%	65%	73%	+	685
	White	53%	61%	70%	69%	78%	+	534
	Black	13%	18%	18%	26%	28%	+	67
	Hispanic	35%	37%	32%	44%	42%	=	19
	Asian	47%	66%	63%	73%	72%	+	65
	Am. Indian	**	**	**	**	**	**	0
	SPED	14%	22%	24%	28%	34%	+	60
	EL	4%	8%	5%	18%	15%	=	19
	FRP	16%	29%	22%	36%	32%	+	83
	Female	47%	58%	60%	NA	70%	+	319
	Male	50%	58%	66%	NA	75%	+	366

Indicator 3 **MCA Science** **High School**	**Subgroups**	**Trend**			**Targets**		**3-yr Trend**	**n 2010**
All students will demonstrate proficiency on the MCA-II and MTAS Science test at EPHS. ** Less than ten students were in this subgroup		MCA/ MTAS 2008	MCA/ MTAS 2009	MCA/ MTAS 2010	Targets 2010	Targets 2011	+ / – / =	n
	All	59%	66%	60%	72%	70%	=	606
	White	61%	68%	62%	73%	72%	=	510
	Black	27%	37%	34%	46%	44%	+	35
	Hispanic	23%	67%	48%	72%	58%	+	21
	Asian	67%	71%	61%	76%	71%	–	36
	Am. Indian	**	**	**	**	81%	**	4
	SPED	30%	37%	25%	43%	35%	–	44
	EL	**	**	**	**	**	**	1
	FRP	25%	44%	35%	53%	45%	+	68
	Female	56%	66%	60%	NA	70%	=	296
	Male	61%	66%	60%	NA	70%	=	310

Indicator 4 Common Assessments High School	Subgroups	Trend		Targets		2-yr Trend	n size 2010
All students will be proficient on the experimental design rubric in each of the high school science courses. ** Less than ten students were in this subgroup.		2009	2010	2010	2011	+/–	n
	All	84%	82%	86%	87%	=	2105
	White	87%	85%	89%	89%	=	1690
	Black	60%	56%	67%	66%	=	172
	Hispanic	66%	67%	70%	75%	=	69
	Asian	86%	88%	88%	91%	=	164
	Am. Indian	**	80%	**	85%	–	10
	SPED	63%	68%	69%	76%	+	166
	EL	27%	38%	**	48%	+	37
	FRP	61%	64%	68%	73%	=	284
	Female	89%	86%	86%	90%	=	990
	Male	80%	78%	86%	84%	=	1115

	Indicator 5 Stretch Activities		2006–2007	2007–2008	2008–2009	2009–2010	4-yr Trend
Stretch	Students will stretch to meet the science standards by applying their scientific knowledge and skills through their work in these science activities: Science Fair Science Olympiad Robotics Team	Science Fair	85	117	165	150	+
		Science Olympiad	N/A	10	33	45	+
		Robotics Team	N/A	10	20	20	+

	Indicator 6 Stretch Courses CMS	Sub-groups	Trend (completed)		Targets		2-yr Trend	n size 2010
			2009	2010	June 2010	June 2011	+/–	n
Stretch	Students will stretch to meet the science standards by completing advanced science courses at CMS: Enriched Science 7 Enriched Science 8 ** Less than ten students were in this subgroup.	All	31%	27%	31%	26%	–	388
		White	31%	27%	31%	27%	=	305
		Black	19%	7%	25%	11%	–	10
		Hispanic	**	**	**	**	**	6
		Asian	42%	46%	42%	46%	=	65
		Am. Indian	**	**	**	**	**	0
		SPED	**	**	**	**	**	3
		EL	**	**	**	**	**	0
		FRP	**	8%	**	13%	+	17
		Female		22%		24%		152
		Male		31%		30%		236

	Indicator 7 Stretch Courses EPHS	Subgroups	Trend (completed)		Targets		2-yr Trend	n size 2010
Stretch	Students will stretch to meet the science standards by completing advanced science courses at EPHS: Civil Engineering and Architecture Principles of Engineering Digital Electronics Intro to Engineering Design Enriched Science 9 Enriched Biology Advanced Biology Anatomy AP Biology Advanced Biology Botany Enriched Chemistry AP Chemistry Enriched Physics AP Physics ** Less than ten students were in this subgroup.		2009	2010	June 2010	June 2011	+/–	n
		All	37%	39%	37%	39%	=	1259
		White	36%	40%	37%	40%	=	1026
		Black	13%	12%	25%	19%	=	33
		Hispanic	20%	16%	29%	22%	=	16
		Asian	74%	71%	74%	71%	=	178
		Am. Indian	**	**	**	**	**	6
		SPED	**	13%	**	19%	+	32
		EL	**	**	**	**	**	0
		FRP	**	18%	**	23%	+	76
		Female		33%		35%		514
		Male		44%		44%		745

Capacity Building

New Science Standards

Beginning this current school year (2010–2011), our curriculum, instruction and assessments in science have been aligned to the new Minnesota State Standards in science released in May 2010. Our students will be assessed by the Science MCA on these new standards in the spring of 2012. From the standards document we learn about the new emphasis on engineering in the standards:

"The 2009 *Minnesota Academic Standards in Science* set the expectations for achievement in science for K–12 students in Minnesota. The standards are grounded in the belief that all students can and should be scientifically literate. Scientific literacy enables people to use scientific principles and processes to make personal decisions and to participate in discussions of scientific issues that affect society (NRC, 1996). The standards and benchmarks describe a connected body of science and engineering knowledge acquired through active participation in science experiences. These experiences include hands-on laboratory activities rooted in scientific inquiry and engineering design. The standards are placed at the grade level where mastery is expected with recognition that a progression of learning experiences in earlier grades builds the foundation for mastery later on. The *Minnesota Academic Standards in Science* are organized by grade level into four content *strands*: 1) the Nature of Science and Engineering, 2) Physical Science, 3) Earth and Space Science, and 4) Life Science. It is important to note that the content and skills in the Nature of Science and Engineering are not intended to be taught as a stand-alone unit or an isolated course, but embedded and used in the teaching, learning, and assessment of the content in the other strands. Each strand has three or four *substrands*. Each substrand contains two or more *standards* and one or more *benchmarks*. The benchmarks supplement the standards by specifying the academic knowledge and skills that schools must offer and students must achieve to satisfactorily complete a standard. Not all standards are found at every grade level" (MDE, 2010).

Systemic efforts and strategies being implemented to improve our students' science performance

Elementary level

- K–5 science teachers were provided content and language objectives training during the science curriculum implementation in August. This training was provided on August 12 and 18 for K–5 science teachers with approximately eighty participants.
- As we transition to a K–6 configuration we will improve alignment between K–4 science curriculum and 5–6 grade curriculum which should improve student performance on the Science MCA.
- As we transition to a K–6 configuration we will work to implement the recommendations of the K–6 Ideas and Possibilities Task Force and incorporate a fifty-minute science block into the daily schedule, as well as emphasize STEM principles in the core curriculum.
- Science literacy is emphasized in the new standards. The new curriculum emphasizes writing in science. Students keep science journals and are expected to gather and analyze data and put their thoughts in written form in these journals. There is a more intentional focus on interpreting graphs and gathering information presented in graphic formats.

Secondary level

- CMS is adopting targeted intervention strategies with specific subgroups in science as they have with reading and math. CMS will continue to focus on closing the gap by paying attention to struggling students through their PLCs, advisory groups, Q-Comp efforts, and professional development investments.
- As a result of the most recent CIC process, high school science classes have a stronger inquiry component than in the past. Beginning with the class of four years from now (this year's eighth graders), the third science credit will need to be in chemistry or physics, so we are programming toward that end.

- The high school is in the third year of an EL science class that introduces students to physical science concepts and builds science vocabulary. This course is team taught with a science and ESL teacher.
- The Science MCA presents logistical challenges at the high school where many students have taken biology in the first semester while the assessment occurs in April during the biology block. The high school is committed to ensuring that all eligible students participate in the MCA this coming spring.

Online assessment issues

- The Science MCA is a computer delivered assessment. During each of the past three years we have experienced technological challenges administering the test. The state recognizes these challenges and is committed to improving the assessment experience.
- We anticipate that with the changes in structure, instructional strategies, and curriculum we will see an increase in science scores in the next three years.

Adopted: June

Revised: January

Monitoring Method: Internal report

Monitoring Frequency: Annually

Eden Prairie, MN School Board

Author's note: Racine is doing a great job of presenting their reports. We have abbreviated the full report to include only one data table to represent the other tables.

Racine Unified School District

Results Monitoring Report

R-2 (Academic Achievement—Reading)

SUPERINTENDENT CERTIFICATION

With respect to Results Policy R-2 (Academic Achievement—Reading), the superintendent certifies that the following information is accurate and complete, and that the district is:

______________	Making reasonable progress toward achieving the desired results
X	Making reasonable progress with the exceptions noted
______________	Failing to make reasonable organizational progress

We assert that the district is making reasonable progress with exceptions

Signed: ______________________________ Date: ____________________

Superintendent

______________ Making reasonable progress toward achieving the desired results

______________ Making reasonable progress with the exceptions noted

______________ Failing to make reasonable organizational progress

Commendations and/or recommendations, if any:

____

____

____

____

Signed: ______________________ Date: ________________

Board President

Racine Unified School District

Results Monitoring Report

R-2 (Academic Achievement—Reading)

Purpose of the Results Monitoring Report:

The purpose of this report with objective evidence is that reasonable progress is being made to achieve the Results identified by the board in Policy R-2 (Reading).

Policy Statement:

Students will achieve academically at levels commensurate with challenging and yearly personalized learning goals. Each student will achieve at or above grade level in the following disciplines:

- Reading
  a. Kindergarten Benchmark:
     At or above the MAP National Norm first grade fall score

b. Grade 3 Benchmark:
Proficient/Advanced score in reading on the WKCE/WAA
c. Grade 6 Benchmark:
Proficient/Advanced score in reading on the WKCE/WAA

- Math
  a. Grade 5 Benchmark:
  Proficient/Advanced score in math on the WKCE/WAA
  b. Grade 9 Benchmark:
  Completion of Algebra with a grade of B or higher; or enrolled in Geometry

- Language Arts
  Writing
  a. Grade 4 Benchmark:
  At or above the District Writing Proficiency Score on the WKCE Extended Writing Sample
  b. Grade 8 Benchmark:
  At or above the District Writing Proficiency Score on the WKCE Extended Writing Sample
  c. Grade 10 Benchmark:
  At or above the District Writing Proficiency Score on the WKCE Extended Writing Sample

- Science
- Social Studies
- Arts—music, visual art, and drama
- Technology
- Physical Education

Students will graduate career and/or college ready, having successfully completed career or technical programs, and/or graduate with an ACT score at or above the state average (22) [North Star Benchmarks].

Priority is focused on reading, writing and math achievement as fundamental to any further achievement.

Interpretation

The Board of Education values that all students, regardless of age, gender, ethnicity, or socioeconomic circumstance, will read at the expected grade level in which they are enrolled or exceed grade-level standards. The board believes that a child's ability to read is an essential skill of learning and therefore gives it a high priority along with math and writing. The board has adopted the North Star with three reading "stations" (sixth grade, third grade, and kindergarten) identified as critical benchmarks in order for all students to achieve the North Star goals of career and college readiness.

Assessments

The following assessments have been chosen by administration to inform an accurate picture of how our students are achieving in reading. These assessments provide some of the important metrics necessary to monitor the progress of students on their trajectory toward becoming career and/or college ready, as envisioned by the North Star.

- WKCE/WAA at third and sixth grades in fall of each school year
- MAP at kindergarten in spring of each school year

Definition of Assessments and Terms

- *Annual Measurable Objective (AMO)*—Percent of students who need to score Proficient and Advanced in Reading and Mathematics as determined by the Wisconsin Department of Public Instruction in adherence to the No Child Left Behind (NCLB) legislation.
- *Cohort Data*—Tracking of student achievement among the same or roughly the same students from year to year. Example—A comparison of fifth graders this year to roughly the same group of students when they were fourth graders.
- *Economically Disadvantaged*—An "economically disadvantaged" student is a student who is a member of a household that meets the income eligibility guidelines for free or reduced-price meals (less than or equal to 185 percent of Federal Poverty Guidelines) under the National School Lunch Program (NSLP).
- *North Star*—A vision of equity and excellence for RUSD student achievement. In spring 2009 a coalition of district stakeholders proposed that the North Star be the shared vision among all employees. This vision shows the pathway from kindergarten to high school graduation including stations along the way that assure success for *all* students. Success upon graduation from high school is defined as career and/or college readiness.

- *NWEA-MAP*—The Northwest Evaluation Association—Measures of Academic Progress are adaptive, computerized student assessments designed to provide immediate feedback to teachers regarding a student's current instructional level.
- *RIT*—Tests developed by NWEA use a scale called RIT to measure student achievement and growth. RIT stands for Rasch unIT, which is a measurement scale developed to simplify the interpretation of test scores. The RIT score relates directly to the curriculum scale in each subject area. It is an equal-interval scale, like feet or inches, so scores can be added together to calculate accurate class or school averages. RIT scores range from about 150 to 300 depending upon the scale and test season. They make it possible to follow a student's educational growth over time.
- *Scale scores*—In the case of the WKCE, scale scores are the translation of raw scores into an equal-interval metric based on Item Response Theory (i.e.—some questions on the WKCE are more difficult/less difficult and should therefore be mathematically weighted) which allows for comparison and computation. The scaled scores for these tests are designed to allow for a comparison of performance across years and grade levels. The scale is a continuum from grade 3–8 and 10. This continuum allows each student's progress towards meeting state performance levels.
- *WKCE/WAA Combined Score*—At a given grade level, this score represents the sum of the percentage of students who score proficient and advanced on the Wisconsin Knowledge and Concepts Exam and the Wisconsin Alternate Assessment at each grade level in which the test is administered.

Data Analysis and Conclusions

- The important measures for analyzing reasonable progress of our students in this report are achievement status (ex.—proficiency score) and achievement growth (ex.—one-year change in average scale scores). Also, we are interested in the degree of change in the achievement gap, especially between black and white students.
- We observe that although we are making progress toward our North Star targets for reading, the achievement gap between white students and other demographic groups remains unacceptable. The achievement gap for black students is of primary concern.
- Cabinet review of achievement gaps using the district North Star Scorecard and other data have led to action steps taken in collaboration with

school staff. Area superintendents and other Administrative Services Center staff have met with each high school principal and representatives from the school's data team to share district-level observations, highlight concerns resulting from this analysis, and inform the work of each school's data team later this summer at the Shared Leadership Academy. A similar process will be followed for middle schools.

Reasonable Progress with Exceptions

1. At the district level, all sixth grade reading groups met their first-year North Star targets. The all students group met their second-year target during this first year. Having met this two-year goal, the target for all students was reset for the 2010–2011 school year for an increase over the 2009–2010 actual score. Overall, an increase of three percentage points in proficiency per year was targeted for all students and white students while an increase of six percentage points was targeted for black, Hispanic, limited english proficient (LEP), low socioeconomic level (Low SES) students, and students with disabilities (SwD). The sixth-grade reading achievement gap between black and white students was narrowed from approximately twenty-four percentage points to seventeen.
2. Three of the third grade demographic groups met their targets. Three other groups improved over the observation period but not to the target level. However, the gap between black and white students widened from approximately twenty-eight to thirty-three percentage points.
3. None of the kindergarten reading groups met their targets. However, five of seven kindergarten groups improved their results. The achievement gap between black and white students widened from approximately twenty-two to twenty-four points.
4. Two-year WKCE cohort comparisons represent positive progress. When comparing the increases in the percent of students among cohort groups in grades 3–4, 4–5, 5–6, and 7–8 who scored in the Proficient or Advanced levels on the WKCE in reading, the percentage point increases are better than the state's performance in reading at all grade spans.
5. In fall 2009, RUSD students achieved the AMO of 74 percent Proficient and Advanced in reading at grades 6, 7, and 8.
6. One-year changes in WKCE scale score means from fall 2008 to fall 2009 are encouraging. Growth in scale score means from grades 3 to 4,

4 to 5, 5 to 6, and 6 to 7 for black, Hispanic, and white students all exceeded the state mean changes.

Challenges

The level of poverty among our students continues to increase and we know that economically disadvantaged circumstances remain a factor in students' readiness to learn. During the 2009–2010 school year, there were 62.3 percent elementary, 56.8 percent middle, and 44.3 percent of our high school students who were identified as economically disadvantaged per their eligibility for subsidized lunch, compared to 57.7 percent, 52.1 percent, and 36.7 percent respectively the previous school year. The State Summary percentage during 2009–2010 was 37.2 percent eligible for subsidized lunch; during the previous year the State Summary was 33.6 percent.

The Annual Measurable Objective (AMO) in Reading, the percent of students who score Proficient and Advanced established by the Department of Public Instruction as an accountability measure under the No Child Left Behind legislation, remained the same in 2009–2010 at 74 percent in reading. This standard will rise again in Wisconsin during 2010–2011 to 80.5 percent.

Targets Identified in the North Star Scorecard

Annual targets are indicated in *italic* type. Over the first year of progress monitoring, we observe some areas where we have met or exceeded our targets. Those cells are indicated with green type. Areas for which the district did increase results but did not achieve the targeted level are indicated in blue type. Areas in which results either remained the same or decreased are in red type.

In selected areas the district not only exceeded our targets but also exceeded targets established for the following year. In those instances the targets have been increased by adding three percentage points to the actual 2009–2010 achievement for each of the next two growth periods. Those increased targets are underlined.

Among North Star Achievement data, the numbers in parentheses are first the total N for that category followed by the N for the score which appears immediately above.

Data-Based Problem Setting—We will improve the reading achievement of sixth grade students from 72.5 percent to 84.8 percent proficient and advanced as measured by the WKCE Reading Test by June 2012.

Grade 6 Reading					
	Percentage of Students				**Vision**
	2008–2009	2009–2010	2010–2011	2011–2012	
All Students	72.5% (1330/964)	78.8% (1359/1071)	*81.8%*	*84.8%*	*100%*
White	83.3% (637/530)	86.5% (670/580)	*89.2%*	*92.2%*	*100%*
Black	59.6% (371/221)	69.6% (335/233)	*71.6%*	*77.6%*	*100%*
Hispanic	64.5% (307/198)	73.1% (327/239)	*76.5%*	*82.5%*	*100%*
LEP	55.4% (178/98)	63.0% (162/102)	*67.1%*	*73.1%*	*100%*
Low SES	61.6% (717/442)	70.3% (805/565)	*73.6%*	*79.6%*	*100%*
SwD	40.4% (184/74)	49.3% (210/103)	*52.4%*	*58.4%*	*100%*

Capacity Building—Strategies for Improvement

Among a wealth of current strategies for improvement of teaching and learning in RUSD, solidifying learning targets at every grade level, raising expectations for all children, and development of a Racine instructional framework will all figure prominently.

These results are from the first full school year of the implemented elementary reading adoption that has focused on differentiated instruction with interventions for students experiencing difficulties. With this program's emphasis on robust vocabulary and a renewed focus on writing districtwide, the results on the WKCE in reading and writing are encouraging.

Increased resources allocated to the RUSD program for early childhood students are anticipated to improve learning for these students. A review of curriculum and assessments will strengthen the use of data-driven improvement tools for early childhood students.

The RUSD Summer School became the North Star Summer Academy this year. The revamped curriculum focused on reading and constructed response problems. Expansion of the number of summer school sites allowed for participation by more students.

The curriculum for the RUSD extended time program, Lighted Schoolhouse, is aligned with that of the district's for reading intervention classes. In addition, Lighted Schoolhouse's academic enrichment classes are aligned to the state standards in reading/language arts. This after-school program utilizes the results from the Measures of Academic Progress (MAP) assessment, a computer-adaptive test, to identify the areas in which children need help in reading. Using this strategy, students who participate in the program have on average doubled their norm RIT growth when compared with students who are not in the program. Extended time, aligned curriculum, and utilizing MAP as a frequent and timely progress monitoring measure have been proven strategies for closing achievement gaps.

The Chiwaukee Academy last August provided a focused start to the current school year. School-wide teams used data to identify areas in reading that became the core of their work with students. The North Star stations and the district scorecard were used to further refine plans from the district level to the classroom level. The first six weeks of school-based efforts are reflected in the WKCE results included in the current R-2 report. However, this effort continued throughout the 2009–2010 school year. The 2011 Scorecard and R-2 will be representative of this year-long implementation of School Improvement Plans. There is still a long way to go, but staff within RUSD are seeing the power of collaboration in the results on the WKCE.

At the August, 2010, Shared Leadership Academy at Chiwaukee, initial components of the instructional management system (IMS) will be ready. The IMS, an online resource, will allow staff to access curricular learning targets, identify appropriate assessment instruments and access essential student data through one interface. The technology refresh, replacement of all district computers, was an important element of this system. It will provide all teachers and staff instant access to these important student data, resulting in the realization of more targeted instruction for individual students.

Appendix C

Dialog with Stakeholders

SAMPLE 1

Author's note: This board was ambitious! We have included its directions to facilitators within brackets below along with the questions they asked. Our only recommendation to the board was to keep questions to a maximum of four to six total in order to maintain a reasonable timeframe of 1.5 hours and to allow for exploration of responses.

Nikkei Concerns: Focus Group Scenario and Questions

The Nikkei Concerns Board of Directors has created a set of client benefits that it believes represents what you, an element of our ownership, want and expect for the clients we serve. We want to discuss these identified outcomes with you, and gather your thoughts about them. [*Present Results policies.*]

1. In your opinion, are these current results appropriate for this organization? Are these the client benefits you believe should drive what we do as an organization? Is anything missing? Are there additional benefits for clients you believe we should be delivering?
2. What do you perceive to be the barriers to our delivering these benefits effectively?
3. Some Nikkei in our community have chosen other providers for the services Nikkei Concerns offers. What would we need to change in order to attract our community members to select NC as the source for these services?

Our demographics are changing in a way that will challenge the Board of Directors to maintain Nikkei Concerns as a viable organization. [*Cite the realities of these demographic changes.*] Given these realities, we would value your opinion about a number of choices.

Let me emphasize that we are not close to answering any of these questions; we have just begun this journey. We truly are barely dipping our toes into the water as we place far-ranging options on the table for a cursory look.

Your feedback will help us decide which options to keep on the table, and which ones to discard as we take the next steps toward redesigning our future:

4. Should Nikkei Concerns maintain its dominant focus on meeting the needs and values of the Nikkei community? If no, should we try to maintain our viability by serving the Nikkei community with a broader array of services that go beyond eldercare? If yes, what services might we consider providing?
5. Should Nikkei Concerns maintain eldercare as its dominant area of service?
6. Should we maintain our viability by serving a broader cultural range of clients?
7. If this organization did not exist, and if you were here to design it, what would you create it to do?

SAMPLE 2

Author's note: Key Communicators is such a simple idea and really quite easy to get up and running. Individual members identify who they think are opinion leaders, they share their lists and identify together whom they agree upon, and then the contacts begin. Establishing this network is much easier than starting new focus groups time and again. That said, both systems can be highly effective.

Key Communicators: A Guideline for Getting Started

Reference: GC-3—board work to link with owners and clients

Purpose: Accessing the grapevine

1. A network of influential people to maintain continuing two-way communication with the board.
2. An opportunity for the board to provide timely, full and first-hand information about the organization to influential people.
3. An opportunity for the board to receive information, insight and counsel from the "community grapevine."

Identification of Opinion Leaders: twenty-five to thirty people identified by the board, people others listen to when they talk about your organization.

Preparing for the First Meeting:

1. Establish: date, time, place.
2. Board members divide the list and personally contact suggested participants by phone, sending a follow up postcard with confirmation of the details of the meeting.
3. Provide refreshments and nametags.
4. Roundtable seating.
5. Board greets and sits with invitees.

Postcard Confirmation Copy: (send after phone contact)

"Thank you for agreeing to be a Key Communicator partnering with our board. We look forward to building a continuing communications relationship with you and the other identified opinion leaders for the next year. Our hope is that you will provide your insight, information and wisdom. In return, we will provide you full and timely information about significant board and organizational issues and concerns. (provide meeting data below)

Meeting: Building and street address

Date and time:

We will begin and end on time!

Contact to confirm: Board Secretary, (name and phone)"

Agenda:

7:00 Welcome and introductions (One board member comfortable with public speaking leads the meeting. You can even rotate the role among board members from meeting to meeting. Remember, this is board work, not staff. Arrange for members to record answers on flip charts at appropriate discussion points.)

7:30 Explain purpose of Key Communicators

"The board has determined it needs to develop stronger connections to the owners it serves. Key Communicators is a tool that has been chosen because of its success with boards across the country.

Each of you has been identified by board members as people who are listened to when you speak. We consider you to be opinion leaders who are sought out by others for more intimate knowledge about various topics.

Our purpose is two-fold: to provide you with full and complete information, and provide a forum for deeper discussion about issues we are grappling with. The second purpose is to ask you to share your insights with us about topics of concern to the board and to contact us as you hear things in the community about the organization. Let us help you respond to rumors, to inaccuracies, and to emerging issues."

7:40 Provide a quick update on current issues (sample issues)

- Board reorganization
- Good news on organizational results
- New end result

8:05 Identify issues members want to hear about and discuss at upcoming meetings

8:15 Ask participants: (do this orally!)

1. Will you meet with us on a regular basis?
2. Monthly? Bi-monthly? Quarterly?
3. Period of time: (do not exceed 1.5 hours)

    Central Location:
    Time of day:

4. Will you agree to receive emails or phone calls as issues or events occur to get full, timely and accurate information?
5. Will you agree to contact us with information or to ask for information?

(Give them a voicemail and email contact.)

8:30 Adjourn, confirming the next meeting as your final piece of business.

SAMPLE 3

Author's note: This county-wide school district undertook a strategic focus group dialog plan several years ago. They were assisted by a top-notch, in-house director of communications. They used this well-designed approach to share the board's first draft of a Citizenship Result, to solicit feedback, and eventually, support for district efforts. We have provided the initial draft of the Result, the protocol, and the board's rework of the Result reflecting what they heard.

Further Development of Citizenship Results Policy

R-3

Policy Type: Results

Citizenship

All students will be responsible citizens and productive participants in their communities.

3.1 Students will demonstrate knowledge of their community, its history and its global context.
3.2 Students will appreciate what they have.

Focus Group Protocol

Introduction: (7:30 p.m.–7:31 p.m.)

Introduce yourself. Explain your role as a facilitator and their role as a participant. Emphasize that your role is to pose the questions, ensure that everyone has a chance to respond, and record their responses (remember write their responses VERBATIM on the flip charts). Stress that we want their ideas and believe that they have the information we need to accomplish our task.

Purpose: (7:31 p.m.–7:35 p.m.) The purpose of the focus group session is to:

- Gain insight into how community members define student citizenship,
- What citizenship behaviors they expect our students to demonstrate, and
- How should we measure whether students are good citizens or not.

Review the draft Citizenship Result above.

Process: (7:35 p.m.–7:36 p.m.)

Explain that you will pose the question and give them some time (about 30 seconds) to jot a few ideas down. Position up front to ensure that everyone has a chance to answer you. Plan to call upon folks for the answers (explain how you will do this). Also, let them know that it's okay to "pass" once when called upon. Make sure you remember to go back and collect their response.

Question 1: (Context setting—frame of reference) (7:36 p.m.–7:46 p.m.)

When you think about being an American citizen today and in the future, how do you define citizenship for yourself? What are some of the values, traits and characteristics of a model American citizen?

After they have exhausted their responses, ask:

Now let's think about an American citizen in our county, specifically, a school district student. Are there other values, traits, and characteristics that you would add to your lists?

Question 2: (Demonstrated behaviors) (7:46 p.m.–7:56 p.m.)

Looking at the list you've just generated, what is it that a student would need to do to demonstrate, what kind of behaviors or activities, do they need to do to show others that they are model or good American citizens?

After they have exhausted their responses, ask:

Do they need to do anything else to show they are good American citizens?

Question 3: (Measurements) (7:56 p.m.–8:06 p.m.)

Now, consider all of your responses and think about the following question. If we want to know about student achievement, we look at test scores and other important measurements. If we want to report to you about student progress and accomplishment of good or model citizenship, what types of information or measurements could we use?

Closing Remarks: (8:06 p.m.)

Thank them for their participation. Explain that we will be conducting sessions just like this one in two other clusters. We plan to collect all of the data, analyze their responses, and look for trends, similarities and differences in communities' expectations. A report will be made available to them when the process is completed. Invite them to stay for the next step of the Linkage Meeting and join everyone back in the cafeteria.

(Revised Result policy, after community dialog sessions)

Citizenship

All students will be responsible citizens and productive participants in their community, their country, and the world.

3.1 Students will Respect People, Position, and Property
Students will:

- Be considerate of others
- Respect authority
- Respect property and rights of others
- Respond to direction in a positive manner

3.2 Students Will Commit Personal Time and Talent to Improve Their Community
Students will:

- Seek opportunities to get involved in their community
- Volunteer time and talents to improve quality of life for others
- Connect academic interests to work and volunteer opportunities
- Build positive relationships with community members

3.3 Students Will Be Civic-Minded and Patriotic
Students will:

- Think globally and have knowledge of social, economic and political issues
- Adhere to and uphold all local, state and national laws
- Understand our political and governmental system
- Promote patriotism
- Participate in the democratic process

3.4 Students Will Value Diversity and Cultural Differences
Students will:

- Appreciate the diverse forces and values that shape their community, country and the world
- Interact productively with people of differing race, age, and gender
- Report racism, bullying, and other inappropriate behavior to school authorities

3.5 Students Will Build Productive Relationships and Group Affiliations Within Their School Communities
Students will:

- Build productive relationships with members of their school community
- Actively participate in school sponsored activities and events
- Serve as a positive voice for the interest and issues of others
- Seek opportunities to effect positive change and reform

SAMPLE 4

Author's note: This campaign is textbook perfect for boards who want to proactively engage their community and engender support.

Board Listening Campaign to Build Support

Mission

Focus on the supporters, the semi-supporters, and the uninformed. DO NOT waste time and energy on the naysayers. Word of mouth is the most powerful and impactful means to communicate.

Goal: To develop communication channels and opportunities to drive a listening campaign to:

1. Inform the public about district initiatives and attributes and ask for feedback;
2. Address misinformation and rumors;
3. Gain support for district initiatives.

Output Objective

1. Inform the public about district initiatives and attributes and ask for feedback and input;
2. Address misinformation and rumors;
3. Gain support for district initiatives through various channels on communications and face-to-face communications to external and internal audiences.

Impact Objectives

1. By May 31, 75 percent of the public feel they are informed and heard by the board and are supportive of district initiatives and the direction of the board, as measured through simple, random phone surveys throughout the summer or given by their child's teacher.
2. By May 31, 80 percent of the staff feel they are informed and heard by the board and are supportive of district initiatives and the direction of the board, as measured through district climate survey.

Target Audience: supporters, the semi-supporters, and the uninformed

- Staff
- Parents
- Community partnerships

Strategies

1. Focus on a push strategy of communications where board members are GOING TO staff and patrons to connect with them
2. Use district channels of communication
3. Measure community opinion and evaluate plan based on pre-measurement of community (May) opinion telephone survey, (October) mid-plan measurement, and post-plan measurement (May). Cost: Estimated $30,000

Internal Communication Tactics

1. Weekly communication message to staff
    - Message from the board—a message from a new board member each week
    - Address positive and negative issues going on
    - We will "stay the course" and continue our duties and expectations
    - Thank you for your hard work
2. Continue the "Unsung Heroes" of our school district program
3. Have one board member attend one staff meeting at each school for a Q&A discussion about allegations and issues going on in the district.
4. Develop a speaker's bureau of teachers who support the district's initiatives. Utilize this speaker's bureau to communicate to the public and internal staff groups.

External Communication Tactics

1. Connect with parent support groups like the PTO, and parent volunteers to host coffees.
2. Schedule one coffee hosted by small groups of patrons where board members attend to complete the three components of the goal.
3. Create a group of patrons who are willing to sign their name to letters to editor for the purpose of completing the three components of the goal. One to three letters to the editor should be published in the local newspaper per week.
4. Board members go to the community to complete the components of the goal through:

- After school care locations when parents are picking up their kids
- School events such as concerts, literacy nights, parent-teacher conferences and back-to-school nights

5. Continue to infiltrate media channels and send press releases to the media regarding board meeting dates, agenda/discussion items, district initiatives, and events where board members are talking to the community.
6. Design a fold-out business card–size marketing piece hand out for the board that states the main goals and mission of the board and contact information.
7. Attend events related to community organizations such as community centers and other communal places.

Communication Department Role

- Design and distribution
- Keep an ongoing calendar of events for the board to attend of internal and external meetings
- Update public opinion dashboard—lessons learned, talking points, main questions/concerns, updates on naysayer communication, telephone survey statistics, schools visited, group discussions, media articles, opinion letters, and so forth
- Manage the telephone survey program
- Manage talking points to the community
- Manage media inquiries
- Assign engagements for speaker's bureau
- Research speaking opportunities
- Track stakeholders, parent groups, and PTO liaisons in the district
- Maintain social media channels

Additional Budget Needed

Telephone Survey $30,000
(Can be justified to community because we want to get community input and figure out where to go from here.)
Board marketing handout $4,000
Additional radio advertising $15,000
(Can be justified to community because we want to attract more students and families for more government funding.)

Appendix D

Agendas for Good Governance

SAMPLE 1

HARRISON SCHOOL DISTRICT NO. 2, EL PASO COUNTY, COLORADO, BOARD OF EDUCATION

Regular Board Meeting:
Date and Location:

1. Convene—5:30 p.m.
   A. Call to Order and Roll Call
   B. Pledge of Allegiance: led by a student from the New Horizons School.
   C. Mission Statement: read by a student from the New Horizons School.
2. Adopt agenda—5:35 p.m. GC-2
3. Showcasing Schools—5:40 p.m. R-1
   Students will make reasonable progress toward one year's academic gain each year, with low achieving students progressing more quickly, in the following disciplines: reading, writing, math, and science.
   A. New Horizons/The Opportunity School/Challenger Program
   Principal's Report: Presented by Jim Reid
4. Superintendent's Report—5:55 p.m. GC-2/OE 8.10
   Provide for the board adequate information about all administrative actions and decisions that are delegated to the superintendent, but required by law to be approved by the board.

A. Achievement Data: New Horizons School /Wildflower Elementary School R-1

Students will make reasonable progress toward one year's academic gain each year, with low achieving students progressing more quickly in the following disciplines: reading, writing, math, and science.

5. Board Development—6:25 p.m. GC-6, GC-6.d

   The board will follow an annual work plan that includes continual monitoring and review of all policies, dialog sessions with community and staff groups, and activities to improve board performance.

   A. Colorado Association of School Boards Fall Regional Meeting Report

   B. Colorado Association of School Boards Fall Conference/Delegate Assembly Report

6. Public Comment—6:45 p.m. GC-3.3

   Initiate and maintain constructive two-way dialog with students, staff, parents, and the citizens as a means to engage all stakeholders in the work of the board and the district.

7. Monitoring Board Performance—7:00 p.m. BSR-5.1

   The board will determine district performance based upon a systematic monitoring process.

   A. Annual Work Plan GC-6

   The board will follow an annual work plan that includes continual monitoring and review of all policies, dialog sessions with community and staff groups, and activities to improve board performance.

   B. Monitoring Schedule GC-6.2c

   Scheduled monitoring of all policies.

8. Superintendent's Consent Agenda—7:10 p.m. GC-2.4

   All administrative matters delegated to the superintendent that are required to be approved by the board will be acted upon by the board via the consent agenda.

   A. Personnel Employment

   B. Financial Statement

9. Board Consent Agenda—7:15 p.m. GC-2.4

   A. *The board will use a consent agenda as a means to expedite the disposition of routine matters and dispose of other items of business it chooses not to discuss.*

   Approval of Minutes—September 7, 2010, and September 23, 2010, Recess (five minutes)

10. Board Debrief of Meeting—7:20 p.m. GC-2.2
    The board will assess the quality of each meeting by debriefing the meeting following its conclusion.
11. Adjourn—7:30 p.m.

SAMPLE 2

Author's note: This agenda was this board's first after it adopted CG. It is remarkable in its ties to policy, use of consent agendas, focus on linkage and board development, and debriefing.

Board of Education Meeting
AGENDA

Pre-Meeting Linkage Conversation: Focus Group 5:00 pm
Topic: R-1 Mega Result and R-2 Knowledge/Academic Achievement

1. Convene 6:30 pm
   Call to order, roll call, establish quorum, Pledge of Allegiance
2. Adopt agenda: 6:31 pm
3. Spotlight GC-3
4. Comment: Public, Board, and Administration GC-3
   Members of the public who desire to address the board on any topic related to board work are welcome to do so at this time. Speakers are requested to limit their remarks to not more than three minutes; to appoint a spokesperson if the concern is a group concern; and to supplement verbal presentations with written reports, if necessary or desired.
5. Superintendent Consent Agenda BCR-3, GC-2
   a) Personnel appointments (legally required board action)
   b) Approve award of contracts (legally required board action)
   c) Approve textbooks (legally required board action)
6. Board Consent Agenda
   a) Approve minutes GC-2
7. Action Item
   a) Adoption of Board Governance Model GC-1
8. Monitor Board Policy (Results) R-1
   a) R-4 Character and Citizenship
   Indicators and Baseline (Internal Report from Superintendent)
9. Monitor Operational Performance OE-18
   a) OE-18 Learning Environment/Treatment of Students BCR-5

10. Monitor Board Performance, GC-3 Board Job Description GC-2,3
11. Board Development GC-8

    Instructive conversation with the district's (ex.) curriculum staff and guest experts about (ex.) academic standards and assessments and their application to board Policy (ex.) R-2, Knowledge/Academic Achievement
12. Board debriefing of this evening's meeting GC- 2
13. Adjourn

Glossary

Baseline: current performance measure that serves as the base against which future progress will be measured.

Benchmark: comparison of one organization's performance against other, comparable organizations.

CEO: Chief executive officer, superintendent, executive director—the board's sole link with the operational organization.

Clients: those persons who are served by your organization; those who receive the benefit of what you do.

Compliance: operating in a manner that meets the standards set by the Operational Expectations policies.

Data: subjective and objective information, statistics, facts, figures, records gathered to document compliance with Executive Limitations or Operational Expectations policies and reasonable progress toward Results or Ends policies.

Formative: information intended to be used for internal, ongoing improvement as opposed to summative judgment.

Governance: the role played by a board of directors in its exercise of power and authority over an organization.

Governing Policy: written values identified by the board to govern four areas:

- *Governance Culture or Governance Process:* values by which the board will self-govern;
- *Board-CEO Relationship or Governance Management Connection:* values by which the board will relate to the CEO, defining delegation of authority and means for establishing CEO and organizational accountability;
- *Operational Expectations or Executive Limitations:* values that establish the standards for the organization's performance, including actions and conditions the board expects to exist and those to be avoided as the CEO makes operational decisions;
- *Results or Ends:* outcomes to be achieved for and by clients.

Longitudinal: data gathered to demonstrate progress over time.

Monitoring: a process that establishes the current state of organizational performance. Operational Expectations monitoring reports document the state of compliance with Operational Expectations policies. Results monitoring reports establish whether reasonable progress has been made toward achieving Results.

Noncompliance: failure to create operational conditions that meet the board's standards.

Organization: any entity created to fulfill owners' needs.

Owners: those whose support is necessary for the organization to survive; individuals whose lives are benefited, either directly or indirectly, by what the organization does.

Policy: the shared value of a board majority that drives action.

Preamble: the opening statement establishing the largest value of any policy. All other sub-parts of a policy are smaller values related to the larger preamble statement.

Reasonable interpretation: staff generated statements intended to assure the board that the values represented by the board's policy statement are understood and can be applied to organizational performance.

Reasonable person: a reasonable person is appropriately informed, capable, aware of the law, and fair-minded such that he is able to render a fair and unbiased decision.

Reasonable progress: organizational performance over time that represents acceptable progress from one point in time to another toward achieving the Results defined by the board. The board, using the "reasonable person standard," according to approved indicators and performance targets developed by the CEO, ultimately defines reasonable progress.

Stakeholders: all individuals and groups of people who are, or might be, affected by the organization's performance; those who hold a stake in what the organization does.

Summative: the summation of, or conclusions reached about, prior monitoring of organizational performance.

Target: a measure of future or predicted performance forecast for each approved indicator.

About the Authors

Linda J. Dawson has more than thirty years of experience as a skilled author, consultant, coach, and facilitator, with a career in teaching and administration, agency public relations, and association leadership. As an executive with the Colorado Association of School Boards, she developed cutting-edge governance training programs, which were highly regarded at the national level. The ensuing demand for her services in other states led to her decision to co-found the Aspen Group in 1993.

Linda attended Westmont College in Santa Barbara and graduated from Rockford College in Illinois. She was director of a three-year project for the National School Boards Foundation on data–based decision-making for boards. She is in demand as a consultant, speaker, trainer, and facilitator, both nationally and internationally. Linda is a widely published author in trade and association magazines. She is an accredited public relations professional (APR) and a qualified Meyers Briggs Type Indicator consultant, certified in strategic planning, and trained by John Carver in his model of Policy Governance®.

Randy Quinn served for thirty years as executive director of two state school boards associations—in Alabama for nineteen years and in Colorado for eleven years. He has written more than four hundred articles for publication in various journals, and has served on the boards of directors of numerous state and national organizations. He benefited from the high visibility of the Colorado board training programs, and co-founded the Aspen Group International in 1993 to extend his work throughout the United States and internationally.

Randy earned his undergraduate degree from Jacksonville State University in Alabama, and his MA and EdD degrees from the University of Alabama.

He is a certified strategic planner and a graduate of John Carver's Policy Governance Academy™.

The Aspen Group International, LLC serves governing boards of all types, principally public and nonprofit boards. Aspen's special area of focus is public school boards, primarily due to the world from which both Linda and Randy came. The company also works with a range of other types of public and nonprofit boards, including cities, counties, self-insurance pools, conservation districts, and elder care organizations.

Since forming the Aspen Group International in 1993, Linda and Randy have consulted with boards in most of the fifty states and others on three different continents, including boards in Morocco, Korea, Borneo, Mexico, Singapore, and Canada.

Their work with boards "on the ground and in the trenches" led them to develop their own governing model variation in 2005. That course of action was taken primarily as a means to meet the specific needs of public boards, whose members face demands and pressures with which members of other types of boards are unfamiliar.

Their governing model, Coherent Governance®, is described in their first book, *Good Governance Is a Choice*, also published by Rowman & Littlefield Education.